The Wreck of the SS *London*

Simon Wills

AMBERLEY

To the Kilimanjaro crew:

Ben, Helen, Kate, Duncan, Liam, Scott, Rob, Long Jon, Karen, Abi, Loraine, Hayley, Harry, Tom, Charlie and of course, Little B.

'Some people dream of worthy accomplishments; others stay awake and do them.'

First published 2016

Amberley Publishing
The Hill, Stroud
Gloucestershire, GL5 4EP

www.amberley-books.com

Copyright © Simon Wills, 2016

The right of Simon Wills to be identified as the Author of this work has been asserted in accordance with the Copyrights, Designs and Patents Act 1988.

All rights reserved. No part of this book may be reprinted or reproduced or utilised in any form or by any electronic, mechanical or other means, now known or hereafter invented, including photocopying and recording, or in any information storage or retrieval system, without the permission in writing from the Publishers.

British Library Cataloguing in Publication Data.
A catalogue record for this book is available from the British Library.

ISBN 978 1 4456 5654 0 (print)
ISBN 978 1 4456 5655 7 (ebook)

Typeset in 10pt on 12pt Sabon.
Typesetting and Origination by Amberley Publishing.
Printed in the UK.

Contents

	Acknowledgments	5
	Preface	6
1	The Ship	8
2	The Owners	20
3	The First Voyages	32
4	The Crew	42
5	The Captain	62
6	The Passengers	72
7	The Final Voyage	84
8	The Sinking	95
9	The Public Reaction	114
10	The Inquiry	140
11	The Aftermath	154
12	The Endings	170
	Appendix: Passengers and Crew of the SS *London*	178
	Bibliography	191

Acknowledgments

This book has proved to be a sizeable and long-running piece of detective work and it could not have been completed without the assistance of so many others who have been kind enough to help me.

Since original documents relating to the events of 1866 are now widely scattered, I have needed a truly global input; from Australia to London, and from Canada to New Zealand, I am grateful for the time and resources that a range of organisations have made available. I would particularly like to thank staff at the following:

National Archives, Kew, London.
Caird Library, National Maritime Museum, Greenwich, UK.
State library of Victoria, Australia.
Trove collection, Australia.
Alexander Turnbull Library, New Zealand.
Maritime History Archive, Newfoundland, Canada.
National Library of Australia.
Maritime Collection, Southampton Central Library, UK.
City of Westminster Archives, London.

For sources of quotations within the text, readers should refer to the bibliography, unless otherwise indicated.

Several friends have persistently urged me to tell the intriguing story of the SS *London* – probably to stop me rambling on about it at social gatherings – and I'm grateful for all their encouragement. I would also like to thank my publishers, Amberley, for their support and input, especially Connor Stait, Ellie Jarvis and Georgina Coleby. However, as always, I owe the biggest debt to my partner, B, who puts up with a writer in the house and all that that entails.

I hope that everyone who has assisted and supported me is pleased with the final result and that you, the reader, can feel transported to what I would call with good reason *the dangerous world of Victorian ships*.

Preface

The story of how I came to write this book would itself probably make a good book. In 2004, I bought an old photograph of the type known as a *carte de visite* from an antiques shop. I bought it simply because I liked the image: three very stern-faced men of character, dating from the mid-1860s – one sat down in the middle and the two others standing flanking him. The text at the bottom of the card states that the men are 'The captain and officers of the *London*'. I now know that this is incorrect and that the photograph actually shows the three passengers who survived the sinking.

Within weeks, by pure coincidence, I came across a slip of paper acting as a bookmark in an old encyclopaedia, which bore the autograph of one 'John King', together with a list of the shipwrecks that this seaman had survived. The last of these was the SS *London*.

I was now intrigued, and determined to investigate further.

So I set about researching this once famous wreck. I also continued to look for memorabilia, and I was fortunate enough to find more – perhaps most notably the magnificent model of the *London* itself, made by a teenage survivor of the disaster. I bought this model from an antique dealer who, like me, admired the sense of movement that it seems to capture. 'It's more like a diorama than a traditional ship model,' he said; 'you can almost hear the rigging sing'. He also pointed out that the 'sea' on which the model sits has been skilfully cut from a single large block of wood, using confident strokes from a sharp, rounded chisel. One of the other survivors of the *London* was William Hart, the carpenter's mate, and I've often wondered if he perhaps carved the sea for Walter. Certainly many survivors kept in touch throughout their lives. We will probably never know.

Even while writing this book I was still unearthing items of interest. I discovered that the Maritime History Archive in Canada held the shipowner's original list of crew and passengers for the *London*'s final voyage, and I found a print of veteran actor Gustavus Vaughan Brooke, who died in the wreck, in an Edinburgh bookshop just days before I sent my final manuscript to the publishers.

Preface

The loss of the SS *London* has, these days, been forgotten – eclipsed by twentieth-century wrecks of much larger ships such as the *Titanic* and the *Lusitania*. Yet when it happened, in 1866, the SS *London* disaster stunned the nation, even though this was an era when shipwrecks were commonplace. The media coverage was widespread and enduring; the public in Britain and Australia were shocked and mournful; and the official inquiry was controversial.

In this book I hope to recapture that lost seafaring world of the mid-1860s. For passengers, crews, and shipowners alike, it was a time of great change, but there was a lax approach to safety that exposed those who travelled by sea to risks. This attitude began with shipowners, and was tolerated by officialdom, yet not communicated to passengers. This was the world into which the SS *London* was launched.

I

The Ship

The SS *London* was a much-acclaimed luxury vessel when it was launched in 1864, but to modern eyes it is a curious mixture of old and new technology: a sleek and elegant sailing ship, yet with a large, smoke-belching funnel amidships. Even though steamships had been in production for two decades or more, shipowners and ships' officers alike still clung doggedly to the need for sail. A significant part of this devotion to wind-powered ships was the long-standing familiarity and traditions associated with the great sailing ship, and a frank mistrust of the newer steam engine. However, sail and steam each had their advantages and disadvantages. If the wind was not blowing in the right direction, blew too strongly, or did not blow at all, then a sailing ship could not make progress. A steamship could cope with all these eventualities and might continue on its voyage through calm or storm. Yet early steamships were not entirely reliable: engines developed faults and stopped working. Engine-driven ships were also more expensive to build; they needed regular refuelling with coal; and they required specialist crewmembers such as engineers to operate them.

Many shipowners liked the speed and the resilience to adverse weather conditions that steamships afforded, but wanted to fall back on wind power when the conditions were right to reduce fuel consumption and to avoid being stranded at sea if the engines failed. The result of this quandary was various types of hybrid ship. Some were clearly steamships that carried sails in case of an emergency, while others were more obviously sailing ships with a back-up engine. The SS *London* fell into the latter class – it was a fully rigged sailing vessel with three masts, but it also carried a small steam engine that drove a single propeller. A contemporary journalist explained that the *London*'s engines were intended 'rather as an auxiliary to aid the ship when becalmed or delayed by adverse winds than as the whole motive power relied on'. Hence hybrid vessels of this kind were known as auxiliary screw steamers.

The SS *London* was 267 feet and 2 inches long, and at its widest point reached 35 feet and 9 inches. So the ship was a long and narrow vessel, in line with the contemporary thinking on fast, clipper-like ships.

The Ship

SS *London* at sea in 1864.

The ship was registered at 1,752 tons – this being a measure not of its weight but of its *volume*, and principally its capacity to carry cargo. This usage of 'tons' to express volume is the conventional way to express the size of commercial ships and it is used throughout this book. However, out of interest, the actual *weight* of the SS *London* when fully laden with cargo, stores, coal and people was about 3,410 tons. Yet, given the size of this ship, it is perhaps surprising to learn that its engine generated a meagre 200 horsepower: many twenty-first-century cars are more powerful than this.

Launch and Sea Trial

The SS *London* was launched from the Blackwall yards on the Thames on 20 July 1864. In a traditional ceremony, involving the breaking of a bottle of wine over the vessel's stern, the ship was christened by Miss Wyndham, the daughter of Colonel Wyndham, who was a friend of the ship's owner. Several thousand spectators cheered as the ship ran off the stocks and slipped down the ways into the river at flood tide.

At launch the ship was simply a hull with decks, and the *London* needed to be fitted out. Masts, sails, spars, and rigging were required, as well as decoration, furnishings, amenities for passengers and, of course, the engines. It is a remarkable tribute to the efficiency of Victorian shipbuilders that all of this fitting out was accomplished in just two months. The whole ship, now complete, had cost the shipping line, Wigram & Sons, the grand total of £80,000: an enormous sum in 1864.

The *London* was ready for its first sea trial on 22 September 1864, when it undertook a return trip from Tilbury, in Essex, to The Nore, a sandbank at the entrance to the Thames Estuary. A host of invited guests, including reporters, were entertained during the voyage:

> She made her trial trip most successfully, conveying a party of nearly 200 ladies and gentlemen, among whom were Sir Henry Young, late Governor of Tasmania, and Lady Young, and many well-known shippers

from the port of London ... Although not in good sailing trim, upon the top of a flood tide she attained a speed of more than eleven knots, with a singular freedom from vibration. Captain Martin, who commands the *London*, is confident of making the voyage to Melbourne, from port to port, in sixty days. The time usually occupied by fast sailing ships is eighty or ninety days.
(*Illustrated London News* 8 Oct 1864)

The captain's confident assertion about a regular sixty-day passage to Australia was unprecedented, and would come back to haunt both him and the ship's owners. Meanwhile, adverts inviting passengers to travel on the SS *London* were already in the press. The ship's maiden voyage to Melbourne was scheduled for 22 October 1864.

Walking the Decks

The SS *London* is the central character of this book. Pictures of the ship and statistics about its size can go some way towards helping the reader to build a mental picture of the SS *London*, but I would like to go a step further and offer you a walking tour of the ship. No deck plans of the vessel survive, but I have been guided by a unique model of the ship made by Walter Edwards – one of the ship's midshipmen who survived the disaster – as well as contemporary descriptions in newspapers and the ship's log.

So, I would like you to imagine that it is 1864 and the SS *London* is on the Thames during its sea trial. You are standing in the open air at the stern of the ship. It's a sunny day, and above you the sky is blue and there is a light wind. Beneath your feet are the planks of the deck in neat parallel lines of timber, stretching away towards the bows. The planks are made from yellow pine – a full 4 inches thick – and are clean and bright because they are virtually new and the crew scrub them every morning. At your back is a white metal rail, which runs all around the deck; it has absorbed the heat of the autumn sun and is warm to the touch.

Model of SS *London*, built by Midshipman Edwards.

The Ship

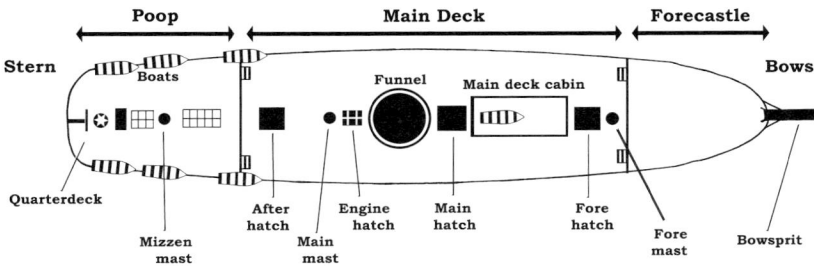

Simplified SS *London* deck plan from above (not to scale).

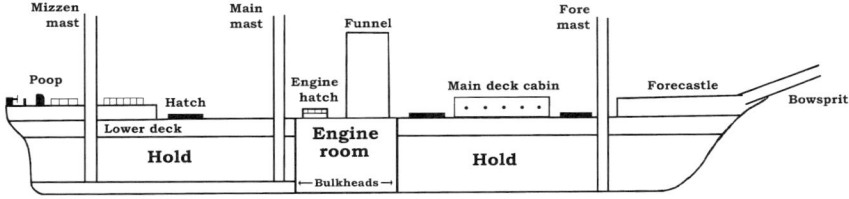

Simplified SS *London* longitudinal section (not to scale).

Immediately in front of you a seaman stands at the ship's wheel. It's an important job for an experienced able seaman, who was often known as the quartermaster. It seems odd to have a helmsman who is about as far from the bows of the ship as it is possible to get, but technology did not yet allow for a ship's wheel to be placed very far from the rudder. At the stern of the ship it is not possible to see dead ahead, so the man at the wheel relies upon guidance from others to determine how to steer. There's an officer of the watch nearby who patrols the deck, keeping an eye on everything, and a series of lookouts who relay information to this officer about potential dangers so that course alterations can be made. The quartermaster and officer of the watch had vital roles and passengers were forbidden to speak to them.

The area around the wheel at the stern is known as the quarterdeck, and is quite exposed to the elements.

You turn around and look over the stern towards the Thames. The first thing you see is a flag billowing out behind the ship – a large, rectangular red flag with a small Union Jack in the top left-hand corner. It's the red ensign, which was only exclusively allocated to the Victorian merchant service in this very year, 1864. Looking downwards you can see the steep sheer side of the SS *London*'s hull. It is made of iron plates riveted together, and is painted black. The water racing away in the vessel's wake is churned up by the single propeller, so that a tail of white stretches away from the ship. At top speed under engine-power alone, the *London* can make a maximum of about 9 knots, but the addition of sails can push this speed up to 11 knots or more. Above the rushing sound of the water, the small engine is still quite noisy and you hear it thudding away somewhere beneath your feet – it's a deep clunking noise that you can feel through the deck.

Red ensign.

Now it's time to move because the wind has changed direction and the dirty blackish smoke from the ship's single funnel has started to blow in your face. The *London* burns coal as fuel, and the smoke has an acrid, slightly sulphurous odour, like the smell of a steam train, which is not unpleasant unless you get a big lungful of it. However, it does quite quickly make clothes dirty with soot if you linger in it.

You decide to walk along the left-hand side of the ship, called the port side. As you pass the helmsman, you see the stout, upright pillar of the binnacle, which holds the ship's compass. After this comes a small, shed-sized shelter with an opening facing towards you, which protects a set of steps leading down into the passenger area beneath you. Beyond this, you almost immediately encounter a large glass skylight with sloping sides like the roof of a greenhouse. The glass is thick, and reinforced to make it resistant to shattering from the inevitable pummelling it will get at sea. This is one of two skylights that let light down into the passenger saloon below. This is followed almost immediately by the rearmost of the SS *London*'s three vertical masts – the mizzen mast. These are manufactured from iron, apart from the timber topmost sections, and are painted white. This mast holds four square sails, one above the other, but also a large, rhomboid-shaped spanker sail on a boom at the bottom, which runs in a fore-and-aft direction. The boom juts out from the mast towards the stern of the ship and is secured by ropes to prevent it swinging dangerously from side to side.

Looking to your left you also spot the first of the *London*'s boats swinging at their davits over the port side. Ships of this period carried various small boats to transport passengers and crew ashore, or for use in case of emergencies. Here you see a lifeboat and a longboat, in line, one behind the other, both painted black and white. There is a corresponding partner to each of them in the same position on the starboard side of the vessel. The *London* had seven such boats in total.

The Merchant Shipping Act specified an arbitrary legal 'volume' of boat space that had to be provided for carrying people when abandoning ship, and this was related to the overall size of the vessel. In the case of

The Ship

The *London*'s poop on Edwards' model, showing quarterdeck, saloon skylights, mizzen mast with spanker boom, and starboard boats. The ship's seven boats were:

Boat	Length	Breadth
Two iron longboats or pinnaces	26 feet	8 feet
Two lifeboats	26 feet	7 feet
One cutter	26 feet	7 feet
One cutter	26 feet	6 feet
One jolly-boat	24 feet	5 feet 6 inches

the *London*, the seven ship's boats amounted to a total carrying capacity of 3,583 cubic feet, which was some 400 cubic feet more than was legally required. This was never intended to provide enough space to accommodate everyone on board in the event of an emergency. It was somewhat fatalistically decided that when a ship went down it would never be possible to save everyone. Hence a very low bar was set in terms of the likelihood of survival in the event of disaster. It is also true to say that shipowners did not want to pay for a lot more boats, and did not like the idea of them cluttering up the ship. Life vests were not supplied at all, and the *London* carried a mere six lifebelts.

You move on, and pass another skylight, which lets more light into the saloon beneath your feet: you can see people milling around in the space below. After this, you come to a short flight of descending wooden steps that takes you down one level to the main deck. The raised area you are leaving is called the poop, and it was restricted to crew and First Class passengers only.

You continue forward along the main deck, passing guests chatting and enjoying drinks. On the main deck the ship's thick hull comes up to the level of your head to form a metal wall, which stops people or anything else falling over the side. This barrier is called a bulwark. You pass a large, square-ish raised area at knee height on your right-hand side. This is the after hatch. The hatchway cover acts as a lid: it can be removed to allow cargo to be lowered into the ship's hold, but it can also be securely fastened ('battened down') during bad weather to stop water penetrating below. In this situation it is common to cover it with tarpaulin as well. In hot weather the hatch cover can be opened to allow air to circulate within the ship.

The lifeboat service had used cork life-vests since 1861, but passenger ships did not carry them.

Hatches allowed entrance to the depths of the ship's hold.

The next mast you come to is the tallest of the three and is called the mainmast. You can just about see the owner's flag flapping away at the top of this mast but it's a long way up – the mast is over 100 feet in length. In order to maintain its strength, it is 33 inches in diameter at the base. The mainmast can hold five square sails and, as you gaze upwards, you wonder how any sailor can remember what all those ropes do. There are so many of them! And how on earth do they manage to scurry around up there on those narrow spars with such confidence, and without a safety harness or any means to save themselves if they fall? The wind has picked up a little and you can hear the ship's 'song' – the sound that the wind makes as it whistles and hums through the taught rigging.

The next construction that meets your eye as you continue walking forward is to prove vital to the survival of the SS *London* during its fateful third voyage. A house-shaped structure, 4 feet high, it has glass panels half an inch thick that admit light into the engine room below. It is 12.5 feet by 9.5 feet. This all-important engine-hatch cover comes just before the ship's

Looking aloft – the seaman had to know every rope and sail.

black funnel, pumping out dark smoke. Made of iron sheets riveted together to form a large tube, the funnel is bolted to the deck and has four thick iron chains or 'stays' to secure it to the hull. Beyond that, there is a small ventilator pipe to let in air, and then another access route to the hold – the main hatch – that also acts as an entrance to some of the Second Class cabins on the deck below.

After this comes the ship's highly polished brass bell, perched on a raised stand and bearing the vessel's name. It is rung to mark the passage of time on board. The bell comes just before the main deck cabinhouse, which is the largest structure on this deck. It is painted white and houses a number of First Class cabins in addition to those found at the stern of the ship, near the saloon that you looked into from above. Some cabins have a small porthole. Balanced on top of the cabinhouse is the smallest of the *London*'s boats – the jolly boat.

Beyond this is the fore hatch and, finally, you encounter the towering white foremast, which like the mainmast can carry five square sails.

To continue your walk, you now need to climb up some wooden steps to reach a raised deck area known as the forecastle (pronounced 'folk-sull'). At the foot of the stairs you notice a door to your right, which is an entrance to some of the cabins for Second Class passengers, together with a communal saloon. There are quarters for some of the crew beneath the forecastle too. Ascending the stairs you come upon a large expanse of open deck where passengers can congregate or enjoy exercise, and you walk across it towards the bows of the ship. The air is more bracing here and devoid of the smell of coal smoke.

You pass the windlass, a rounded column-like structure used to raise the anchor, and then, stretching out ahead of you, pointing the way into the

The Ship

Amidships – with funnel, main hatch, and main deck cabin. (The jolly boat on top of the cabin is missing from Edwards' model.)

waves like a large bony white finger, is the bowsprit, which can carry up to four elongated triangular sails. You can go no further. You peer over the side and can just see the ship's anchors fastened to the sides, but you already know that the *London* does not carry a figurehead: they seem to have gone out of fashion. You've now walked the entire length of the ship. At a gentle pace the whole distance of 267 feet took you perhaps two minutes. So it is a small space in which to be confined for two months or so on a journey to Australia.

Bows of the SS *London*.

You turn around, and walk back down the steps to the main deck; you pass the funnel again, and reach the bottom of the steps that would take you back up to the poop. You don't ascend, but open a wooden door next to the steps that admits you to the First Class saloon. This is a large area where passengers travelling First Class can congregate and enjoy each other's company – a welcome break from being confined in a small cabin. It is pleasantly decorated, with elegantly patterned and polished woodwork adorning the walls, as well as a selection of oil paintings and murals. There is a piano, padded chairs screwed to the deck, a clock and barometer, cushions, rugs on the floor, a few potted plants, and even a stove to warm the area on cold days. Dominating the space is a long table, around which the passengers will eat, as the saloon is both dining room and drawing room. Steps connect this upper saloon to a lower saloon on the deck below. A steward stands in attendance in case any of the passengers should require assistance, or perhaps a little something to drink. The forecastle saloon that you passed earlier is decorated with slightly less refinement, but is still a very pleasing sight.

When seated in the saloon you could for a moment believe that you were on land, if it weren't for the motion of the ship. The standard of decoration throughout the ship is of a high order and many passengers are attracted to the *London* because of the luxury of the surroundings. Two months at sea is a long time, and anything to make the long journey more bearable is most welcome. You can now appreciate the value of the two large skylights above that you saw when on the poop, as they let in a great deal of light and make the space bright and cheerful.

The First Class passenger accommodation is to be found running around the stern of the ship as a series of cabins in a horseshoe shape with the saloon at the centre. These stern-most quarters or state rooms are deemed the most prestigious, largely as a result of tradition. In earlier times, the captain had customarily had a large cabin at the stern of the ship and passengers now sought this distinction. However, the stern is more susceptible to the rocking of the ship than the centre, and it is also closer to the propeller and so can be noisier. You take a peek into some of the First Class cabins. They are all very small – about 6 or 7 feet square – with one or two narrow bunk beds, a lamp and a shelf. There is also a wash stand with a mirror, and stewards will supply you with a jug of warm water every morning and evening for washing and shaving. Most of the rooms can accommodate two people, but there is generally only enough room for one person to stand up and get dressed at a time. The passengers bring all their possessions for the voyage on board in a large trunk, which they live out of for the duration of the voyage, and this is stowed under one of the bunks. There are hooks on the walls so that clothes can be hung up.

You retrace your steps to the saloon and take the steps that lead you downwards. Beneath the main deck, which you are just about to leave, is one more deck – the lower deck. As you descend, the air takes on a warm, musty aroma – a smell of confinement. The atmosphere is stuffy because there's much less ventilation down here and it's rather gloomy: the only light

The Ship

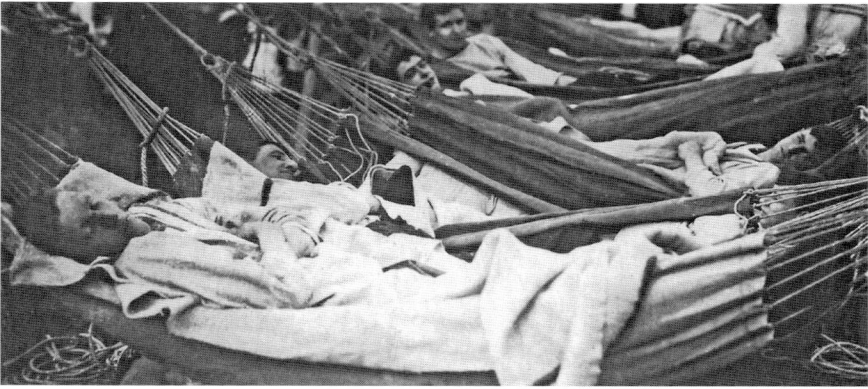

Sailors in hammocks.

comes via lanterns that are hung up around the ship. They carry a naked flame within a glass casing and burn oil, producing a thick, fatty smell. The space between decks is quite high – about 7 feet – so you have plenty of room to walk upright without banging your head.

On this level can be found more cabins for Second Class passengers – most of them roughly amidships and usually accessed via a ladder that leads down from the deck above via the main hatch. There are also cramped berths for Third Class passengers down here, and Steerage passengers would be accommodated in hammocks slung at night in an open, dormitory-style area.

The lower deck houses the galley, where food is prepared, and the top of the 36-foot engine room, which extends downwards as a single space to the lowest reaches of the ship. At the bottom sit the engines. The crew's quarters are mostly found towards the bows – cabins for senior men, and an open area containing hammocks for the rest. The crew are accommodated in the foremost parts of the ship where the vessel's motion is most pronounced as the bows plunge into the waves. You can hear more of the creaking of the ship down here and the sounds of the ships' engines are much louder; it also feels claustrophobic because of the gloom.

The only other space that you have not explored is the hold. This is a huge area beneath the lower deck up to 24 feet deep. Here, cargo is stored in four large compartments, together with passenger luggage not required on the voyage, but only crewmen are allowed to enter this area.

2
The Owners

The SS *London* was owned by a once famous shipping line called Money Wigram & Sons. The founder of this company, the unusually named Mr Money Wigram, inherited a shipping business from his distinguished father, Robert Wigram. To understand the business ethos and attitude of the SS *London*'s owners, it is necessary to know something of the history of Robert Wigram and the means by which Money Wigram & Sons came into being.

Founding Father

Robert Wigram was born in Wexford in 1744. He never knew his father because he died at sea when Robert was just two years old, and so he was brought up by his mother and an uncle, who was a doctor. Aged eighteen, Robert was packed off to London to gain a medical qualification and, after completing his training, he became a surgeon aboard a ship of the

Robert Wigram.

Honourable East India Company in 1764. He worked for the company for eight years, but an eye infection in China damaged his eyes to the extent that he became partially sighted and, as a result, he was forced to relinquish his seagoing career.

However, Robert was only in his late twenties, and a very energetic and resourceful man. Casting around for a new way to use his medical knowledge, he set himself up in business as a drug merchant, importing medicinal ingredients from all over the world. His company was an almost immediate success, and quickly earned him a considerable income.

It is often remarked that the East India Company inspired great loyalty among its employees, and Robert was no exception. He wanted to invest his new wealth, and he chose to become an owner of East Indiamen, the name given to ships of the East India Company. Rather charmingly, the managing owners of company ships were at this time referred to as ships' husbands. His first investment came in 1778, when he purchased a share in the East Indiaman *General Goddard*, and the number of his ships grew until within only a few years he became the company's leading husband. This was significant enough, and yet his financial links to the East India Company did not end there. Importantly, Robert also acquired businesses that supplied the company with provisions, but his most significant asset would prove to be his control of the Blackwall shipbuilding yard on the Thames.

The Blackwall yard was one of many shipbuilding concerns on the Thames in the eighteenth and early nineteenth centuries, but it was by far the biggest. Between 1750 and 1825, it built eighty-nine ships for the East India Company alone. In 1790, the yard built the first ship at Robert Wigram's personal instruction – the *True Briton*.

Robert was a shrewd businessman and he became enormously rich, but he embraced many other roles in addition to his shipping interests. He was

Blackwall yards in 1824.

Walthamstow House, Essex, home of Robert Wigram and family.

twice a member of parliament, created a baronet in 1805, and appointed High Sheriff of Essex in 1812. A staunch opponent of slavery, he was also a lieutenant-colonel commanding the 6th Loyal London Volunteers. Yet, despite his many achievements and a busy career, Robert was a devoted family man and the father of a remarkable twenty-three children. He named one of his sons after his close friend, William Money, and thus the uniquely named 'Money Wigram' was introduced into the world.

At the grand age of seventy-four, even Robert's seemingly inexhaustible fount of energy began to run out, and he decided to retire. It was 1819, and Robert relinquished control of the Blackwall yards to two of his sons – Money Wigram and Henry Loftus Wigram – and to his business partner, George Green. When Robert died in 1830, the control of the yards was split between these same three men. Quite apart from his freehold estates and the numerous large sums of money that he had regularly given to his children during his lifetime, he bequeathed an impressive £400,000 to his heirs. Although the two Wigram brothers technically shared ownership of their side of the business, it was always Money Wigram that was in charge.

Money Wigram

Money Wigram had married Mary Turner in 1822, a woman twelve years his junior and the daughter of a business associate of his father's. They had eleven children, three of whom would follow Money Wigram into his merchant shipping business.

Like his father, Robert, Money Wigram was an energetic man who welcomed additional responsibilities. He was a director of the Bank of England, for example, as well as a director of the East India Dock Company (a predecessor of what later became the Port of London Authority). He was also a freemason, and involved with a number of charities, including those for educating under-privileged children.

Through his family, Money Wigram was well connected with all levels of high society – politicians, businessmen, financiers, the armed forces, the church, and the landed gentry. Apart from his own links with the East

Above left: Money Wigram as a young man.

Above right: Money Wigram's brother Joseph was Bishop of Rochester.

India Company through his father, his many brothers stood him in good stead with social connections. His eldest brother, Sir Robert Wigram, was a baronet, former MP, and director of the Bank of England; Sir James was a judge with connections to the privy council; Octavius was an insurance underwriter for Lloyds of London and sat on the committee of Lloyd's Register of Shipping; Joseph was Bishop of Rochester; Henry was co-owner of Wigram & Green and was a Tory MP; William and John were directors of the East India Company, but William was also an MP; and finally George was a biblical scholar who helped establish the Plymouth Brethren. Many of Money Wigram's children, nephews and nieces married into influential families too, and pursued significant careers in their own right.

Money Wigram & Sons

A major part of the initial commercial success of Robert Wigram, his son Money Wigram, and his partner George Green came about because of their relationship with the East India Company. The company previously had a complete trading monopoly with the Indian subcontinent and East Asia, and this rankled with British merchants, who resented the commercial opportunities that were being denied them. Eventually, in 1813 most of the company's monopoly on Indian trade was revoked by Parliament. This opened up ports such as Calcutta (modern Kolkata), Madras (Chennai), and Bombay (Mumbai) to other shipping lines. Wigram & Green grabbed the opportunities – taking passengers and British goods to India, and bringing back valuable Indian cargoes of spices, cloth and other goods. They expanded their fleets to meet demand, purchasing ships and building them.

Wigram & Green built ships for various shipping concerns, but they also built for themselves. By the early 1830s their yards were employing as many as a thousand men. Although a single company in legal terms, in practice the part of the shipping yards run by the Greens built ships that were managed by the Greens, and the Wigrams built ships for the Wigrams. Nevertheless, they operated under a single flag, which has an interesting history. In 1824, the Greens had purchased a ship called the *Sir Edward Paget*, which was commanded by a former Royal Navy officer, Captain Geary. Arriving at Spithead, Portsmouth, the ship was flying the English flag or St George's Cross – a red cross on a white background. The port admiral sent his lieutenant on board to enquire why the ship was flying a flag that at the time was traditionally reserved for an admiral. When the Royal Navy realised that a mere merchant ship had dared to fly this flag, orders were given for it to be taken down immediately. Perhaps unwilling to be told what to do on his own ship by his former employer, Captain Geary quickly instructed that a square blue handkerchief be sewn over the centre of the red cross. When the flag was re-hoisted a few minutes later, the Navy were unable to object. This makeshift flag became the official flag used by all Wigram & Green ships thereafter.

Meanwhile the once powerful East India Company continued to decline, and its slow death became an inevitability by 1833, when it lost the remainder of its trading monopolies in India and with China. After 1832 no new ships were officially built for the company, and many of its existing vessels were sold off in the ensuing years. The writing was on the wall. However, the Wigram & Green partnership continued to construct ships at Blackwall to a broadly similar design, but for other customers. They could no longer be called East Indiamen, so a new name arose in the 1830s – that of the 'Blackwall frigate'. Like the East Indiamen they were

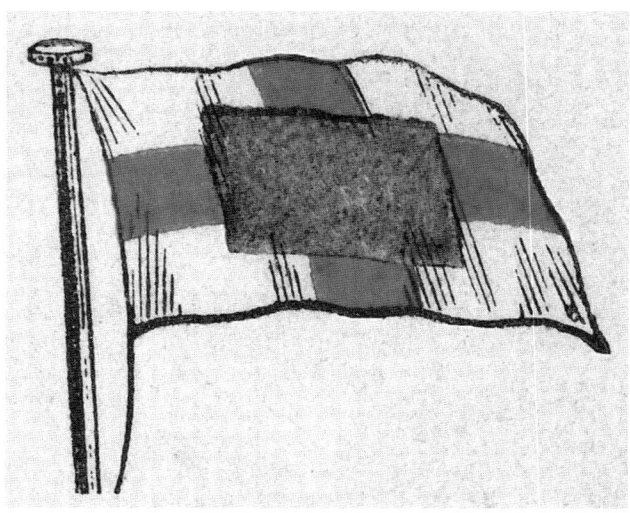

The flag of Wigram & Green.

three-masted, square-rigged, fast sailing ships with black and white hulls. They bore a similarity to the Royal Navy frigates of the time, some of which were also built at Blackwall, and this is probably how the nickname came into being.

The long-standing monopoly of important trade routes by the East India Company had led to complacency and abuse of power by its staff, and many had grown wealthy on profits that were deemed excessive. Their ships were over-manned, slow, small, and expensive to run. In short they were inefficient, so there was plenty of scope for private shipping lines to improve the operation of the old East India Company routes by using larger, faster,

An East India Company ship, *Thames*.

Blackwall frigate.

and more economically run ships. Trade was the lifeblood of the British Empire – merchant ships connected all parts of the Empire together – and by opening up trade routes to competition the government aimed to improve the choices available to merchants and travellers, and to decrease costs. It is important to realise that, although passenger fares were a welcome source of revenue, it was cargo that generated the majority of the income for shipping companies. So all Money Wigram ships carried both passengers and cargo, and the more cargo that could be squeezed on board the better, as it increased the profitability of the voyage.

As the East India Company continued to shrink, many of their crews, officers, and captains came over to shipping businesses like Wigram & Green's, and brought with them the ethos of that old institution – the discipline and good seamanship certainly, but they also anticipated certain standards aboard ship. Crews were large; the officers were gentlemen; rations were of the best quality; and there was a general expectation of a comfortable life on board ship. The new shipping lines that employed them met these requirements within reason, but they were commercial companies with an eye upon the profitability of their enterprises and so cut back where they could. However, even as late as 1849, the East India Company legacy was still impacting: Green's ship the *Alfred*, of only 1,291 tons, had a crew of eighty men including five mates, which was considered notably excessive even at the time.

In 1843 the legal basis of the partnership between the Greens and the Wigrams came to an end and the Blackwall yards were divided. The western half was now owned by the Wigrams, who created a new business called Money Wigram & Sons. By degrees, three of Money's sons joined him in running the business: Charles, Clifford, and Robert. Meanwhile the eastern part of the original Blackwall yards now belonged to Richard ('Dicky') and Henry Green, who established R. & H. Green & Company Limited, better known as Green's Blackwall Line. Wigram & Sons kept the existing company flag, whereas the Greens modified it so that the red cross of St George sat on top of the blue square rather than behind it.

Money Wigram was keen to make a name for his new company in comfortable and speedy voyages to selected destinations. He decided

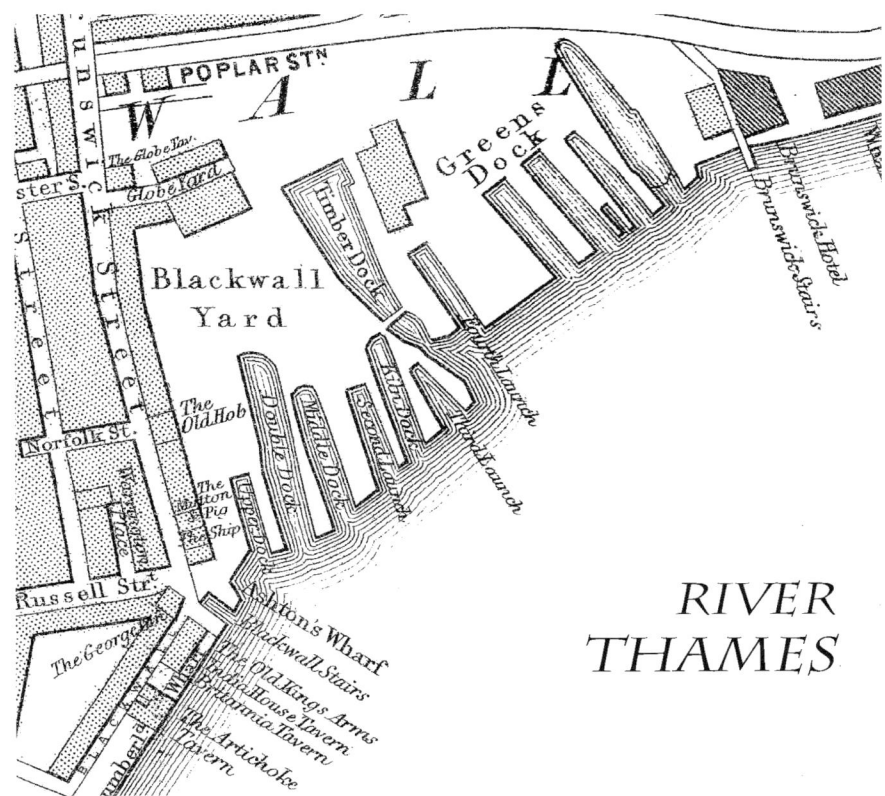

Blackwall yards owned by Wigrams and the Greens' yards next door.

to continue to focus on India, an important part of the British Empire where many UK citizens sought business opportunities, employment with the military and civil service, and the chance to explore the enigmatic subcontinent. However, Money Wigram also targeted the rapidly growing colonies of Australia and New Zealand as important destinations. Emigrants, and especially the Victorian gold rush in Australia in the early 1850s, helped to considerably expand interest in these routes. In the days before the Suez Canal opened in 1868, ships sailing to any of these destinations had to go a far longer way around, via the southerly tip of Africa, so some Money Wigram vessels called at South African ports en route.

In the early 1850s, many shipowners were impressed by new designs of sleek and speedy sailing ships known as clippers. These lofty ships had very tall masts, great spreads of sail, and long, lean hulls with a knife-like bow. They were said to 'go at a good clip' – in other words they were fast – and this is how they got their name. Some British builders had developed clippers as far back as 1830, but the Americans perfected the designs that were capturing attention by the 1850s. The British were quick to copy their ideas and soon clipper ships were common long-distance trading and passenger ships.

Clipper ship *Cutty Sark* was built in 1869.

Clippers were built for speed, and captains vied with each other to get the very best out of their ships. On board these vessels, passengers and crew often wondered at their captain's determination to take their ship to the very limit of its potential. Rigging straining, sails struggling, and the deck heeling over at an angle of 45 degrees – and yet every captain felt impelled to pursue an all-out performance. Passengers and employers judged captains by the speed of a ship's passage: faster vessels could charge passengers more but would still have no trouble filling every berth, even if the ship's crews sometimes felt their captain sailed too close to the edge of safety.

In the early 1850s, Money Wigram & Sons decided to expand their shipbuilding facilities by opening a separate yard at Northam in Southampton, which would have easier access to timber and so would build mainly sailing ships. From this point their business expanded rapidly and, by about 1860, Money Wigram & Sons had a large fleet of about thirty sailing ships, with many named after English counties: *Devonshire*, *Kent*, *Norfolk*, *Lincolnshire*, *Yorkshire* and so forth.

For two decades, fast sailing ships like the clippers were the apogee of sailing technology and elegance, and they continued to operate alongside a different kind of vessel, which was still evolving: the steamship. But steamships had not yet reached their zenith; when they did, the sailing ships would become redundant.

Advances in Shipbuilding

Three innovations were to shape the future of the shipping industry in the early-to-mid Victorian era. The first of these was the steam engine.

Wind-powered ships had to wait for a favourable wind to set sail and were helpless in a storm, but a steam engine could make progress in adverse weather conditions. Early steamships carried large paddlewheels on either side of the ship, which greatly increased the speed of sea travel. Brunel launched his steamship the *Great Western* in 1838, and the travelling public were astounded when it started to ply the route from the UK to the USA in as little as twelve days. Previously an Atlantic crossing took at least a month and often nearer to six weeks. The reliability of steam also meant that ships could adopt regular, scheduled departure times, and thus the era of the ocean liner was born.

The second development that revolutionised the industry was the propeller. The paddlewheels used on many early steamships were large and cumbersome, and prone to mechanical failure. The propeller was much cheaper to manufacture and more energy efficient, so that smaller engines were required. It also took up less space and provided greater manoeuvrability. The inventor of the screw propeller, Francis Smith, received little financial remuneration for his invention, despite taking out a patent. However, in 1856, a group of shipowners subscribed to a fund to reward Smith. Money Wigram, for example, personally donated £50.

The third innovation that helped forge the way ahead for shipowners was the use of iron hulls. Iron was much heavier than wood, but it was stronger and allowed construction of larger ships. Bigger vessels meant more space for both passengers and cargo, and so voyages could become more profitable.

Money Wigram & Sons were innovators when it came to the process of building ships. In 1849, for example, they were one of the first shipbuilders to employ steam-powered machinery to cut ship's timbers, which improved efficiency and reduced wastage and costs.

However, when it came to ship design, Wigram were quite traditional, though not alone in this. Despite the advantages of steam-driven vessels, many ship-owners and captains were still seduced by the nostalgia of the old sailing ships and mistrustful of new steam technology, which, to be fair, was initially sometimes unreliable. The sailing ship evoked certain traditions, which were integral to the history and image of Money Wigram & Sons and its captains. There was a great pride in being a shipping line that had its roots in the East India Company, and the Wigrams were determined to provide an unequalled yet traditional service. In the early 1850s, for example, the Wigram ship *Kent* on the Australian run had regularly raced the *Marco Polo*, which was owned by rivals Blackball Line, to the thrill of the passengers on both ships. The excitement of crews on well-designed ships harnessing the pure power of the wind seemed to be what true seamanship was all about. Hence steam took over from sail on a very gradual basis over a period of a few decades.

The Wigrams had built steamships for other customers, but they had never built one for themselves. During the 1830s the Wigram & Green partnership constructed steamships at Blackwall. They built the paddle steamer *Countess of Lonsdale* for the General Steam Navigation Company in 1836, and experimented with fitting a steam engine into an East Indiaman, but somehow the time had never been right for Money Wigram's own ships to adopt this approach.

The growth of Money Wigram's commercial endeavours are shown by the extent of his personal household staff. In 1841, he and his family lived at Wood House, Wanstead, and employed six servants, but in 1860 he purchased a bigger residence: Moor Place in Much Hadham, Hertfordshire. Within a short space of time Moor Place had been refurbished and enlarged, and was described as a 'mansion' employing thirteen servants: a butler, housekeeper, footman, ladies' maid, coachman, kitchen maid, scullery maid, stable helper, labourer, gardener, garden labourer, and two housemaids. Money Wigram clearly enjoyed his new home and in 1862, aged seventy-two, he decided to retire and live out his days in this opulent residence.

Sailing ships were still very common in the mid-1860s, and this was an era when elegant clippers raced each other across the oceans like giant yachts. However, with Money Wigram himself now retired and a healthy bank balance with which to work, his sons decided that a new direction was required to keep them ahead of the game, since competition on the Australia route was becoming fierce. What was the one factor that made people choose one shipping line over another? The answer was simple: *speed*. No passenger wanted to spend longer on a ship than he or she needed to; no buyer wanted to wait three months for a cargo if they could only wait two. Steam had become more reliable and it enabled a vessel to leave port even when the wind was in the wrong direction, to cruise across breathless oceans with no wind at all, and to power its way through stormy waters. If the Wigrams could construct a fleet of steamships, they would wipe weeks of the journey time to Australia and dominate the route.

Money Wigram in retirement.

An 1860s clipper under full sail has clear similarities to the SS *London*.

It was decided that the company would launch one steamship to test the waters, as it were, and the first ship with engines to fly the Wigram flag was to be called the *London*. In 1832, they had introduced a sailing vessel with this name, which operated very profitably on the run to India and New Zealand for fifteen years. As was often the case in the merchant service, and the Royal Navy too, the names of popular ships were frequently recycled. Besides, reusing the name of a successful ship was said to be lucky...

Everything was set for the *London*'s maiden voyage and great things were expected of her. After all, Captain Martin had predicted that he would reach Melbourne in sixty days.

3
The First Voyages

Money Wigram & Sons were pleased to have a VIP on board for the *London*'s first voyage to Australia in October 1864. Sir Daniel Cooper was former speaker for the Legislative Assembly of New South Wales. Other passengers joined the vessel in London, Gravesend or Plymouth before the ship headed into the Atlantic.

The maiden voyage of the SS *London* should have been an exciting event, but it proved to be a miserable affair for Captain Martin. It started with a minor annoyance. At the beginning of the voyage one of the seamen, Charles Holland, perhaps having taken advantage of the ladies of the port of London, was diagnosed with syphilis and was unable to work for six days. This was not unusual at the time, as venereal diseases were common, but it left the crew one hand short.

More seriously, on 30 October a fire broke out because some of the coal had been stored too near to the hot engines. Thankfully it was extinguished within

Sir Daniel Cooper.

an hour and a half of its discovery, but it happened again three days later. Fire on a ship at sea can rapidly overwhelm a vessel. Captain Martin would have been all too aware of ships such as the notorious RMS *Amazon*, which twelve years before had caught fire and blown up on her maiden voyage. The captain ordered that bags of coal be stored on deck to prevent repetition: a noisy and messy job that can hardly have impressed the passengers, particularly since it would have reduced their already limited room for movement. Fortunately, it had the desired effect and there were no more fires.

For the passengers there was a lot to get used to. The first problem was seasickness. As soon as the first rough seas were encountered, the majority of passengers would start to be sick and this would last for a few days until people became used to life at sea. The motion of the ship also caused a second problem – finding your sea legs. As the ship was buffeted by wind and waves, passengers were caught unawares and fell over or collided with parts of the ship – so minor injuries and a bit of discomfort were to be expected. Finally, passengers had to get used to sleeping at sea. Passenger Samuel Smiles on a Money Wigram ship in 1869 explains:

> I cannot find room to extend myself, or even to turn. I am literally 'cribbed, cabined, and confined'. Then there are the unfamiliar noises outside – the cackling of the ducks, the baa-ing of the sheep, the grunting of the pigs – possibly discussing the novelty of their position. And, nearly all through the night, just outside my cabin, two or three of the seamen sit talking together in gruff undertones. I don't think I slept much during my first night on board.

One of the *London*'s former passengers described his Second Class berth as small and cell-like, so there was little room. However, in time passengers

The steamship *Amazon* ablaze in 1852.

adapted to life on board and gradually got to know one another and key members of the crew as well.

The ship crossed the equator on 11 November and all was well, but tragedy was to come in the middle of the South Atlantic, as recorded by the captain in the ship's log of 21 November 1864:

> 6 a.m. Strong wind, hard squalls, heavy rain with a very high head sea. At 8 a.m. increasing. Shortened sail to topgallants. Carried away the jib stay. At 10 a.m., ship pitching violently.
>
> James Chilvers (boatswain) and Henry Darnford (AB [able-bodied seaman]) were on the jib boom clearing away, when the ship gave a very heavy plunge burying the forecastle and jib boom completely under water. On her rising we found Henry Darnford had been washed overboard. Squared the mainyard immediately and lowered the starboard boat with Robert Harris (chief officer), John Clarke (AB), Giovanni Ghotte (AB), Richard Collins (AB), Richard Cotter (AB), James Rayner (AB); and on lowering she struck against the ship's side with great violence. Ordered a second boat to be got ready for lowering. The first boat got clear of the ship's side and apparently without damage. We therefore thought that lowering a second boat would be an unjustifiable risk with such a heavy sea, so kept all fast. Ordered steam to be got up immediately as the ship was driving very fast to leeward. Wore ship. The boat was seen distinctly by several persons and then suddenly disappeared. When the steam was up, steamed in the direction in which she was seen and reached the place. Did not see her. Steamed in different direction in search until night coming on. We came to the conclusion she must have foundered. Considered further search useless in consequence of the deviation of the compass being so irregular at different points. We therefore set the topsails and hauled close to the wind, it being ESE.

The loss of seven crewmen in such circumstances must have distressed Captain Martin, especially losing his second-in-command. In newspapers these events were later reported to have 'thrown a general gloom over the whole passage'. But did the captain do enough to try and save his men? If he

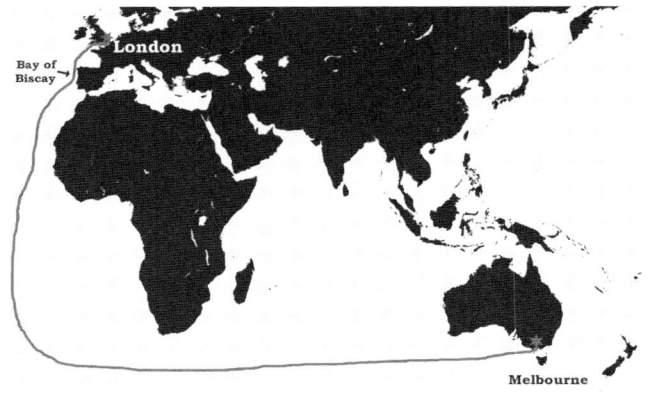

The SS *London*'s route to Melbourne.

hadn't made an announcement to the press about trying to get to Melbourne in sixty days, he might have felt under less pressure for a speedy passage and so stayed longer to continue the search. Perhaps another captain would have hove to overnight and left lights ablaze on the ship hoping that a ship's boat would have something to aim for in the darkness. The *London* had many lanterns on board as well as flare rockets and signal guns.

It is also worth noting that Captain Martin seems to have relied entirely upon his sails to navigate the storm. A more experienced steamship commander would have engaged his engines earlier since they were less adversely affected by strong winds. As it was, the delay in switching to steam power meant that the *London* could not hold her station, was forced away from the ship's boat, and so lost contact.

The 21 November was to prove the only day of bad weather on the entire voyage, and the SS *London* steamed on. However, the ship was obliged to make an unscheduled detour to Cape Town on 5 December because so many of the live sheep needed for the voyage had died and the captain had to buy more. He was successful, and also recruited six able seamen to replace his lost men. The ship departed on the 7th, but there was an unusual incident four days later: Thomas Brydges, the captain's personal cook, was arrested and confined to his quarters for refusing to undertake his duties. He said he had no-one to wash up the dishes despite the sculleryman and the baker agreeing to assist him. The following day he still refused, and was reduced in rank and pay as punishment ('disrated'). Was this a sign of a wider discontent among the crew regarding their captain, and the way he had all too quickly abandoned his crewmen adrift?

Eventually on 3 January the *London* reached Melbourne. The journey had taken sixty-eight days from Plymouth (seventy-three days from departing the Thames estuary) – so considerably longer than Captain Martin's anticipated sixty days. However, on one occasion the ship had managed an impressive 396 miles in a twenty-four-hour period so he knew his ship had potential. Nonetheless, the First Class passengers seemed to have appreciated his efforts at least, as an Australian newspaper reported:

> On arrival, the saloon [First Class] passengers presented Captain Martin with a handsome address, expressive of their thanks for the hearty zeal and ability shown by him, and also expressing the greatest sympathy for the loss of Mr Harris, who was universally respected.
> (*Ballarat Star*, 4 Jan. 1865)

But at this stage the captain was undoubtedly more concerned about official reaction to the loss of his crewmen in the ship's boat. As soon as the *London* docked, the details of his actions became quickly known and criticism began to spread. There were multiple cases of his crewmen being absent without leave and of drunkenness. Some men even refused to work. Eight members of the crew were discharged 'by mutual consent', including the rebellious cook, Thomas Brydges; a further ten men that Captain Martin would like to have retained asked to be discharged. Among these, the loss of his third mate, Thomas Catley, must have been a particular blow. There were also a large number of desertions over the ensuing days: a remarkable twenty-five in total. Of the men who stayed, two were repeatedly reprimanded for drunkenness. The *London*'s remaining officers busied themselves trying to recruit replacement crew at Melbourne.

In the midst of all this criticism and the desperate attrition of discontented crewmen, there came dramatic and unexpected good news: chief officer Robert Harris and the five seamen in the boat had been picked up after thirty-two hours afloat in an open boat. Captain Martin's log records the arrival of this information in the calm and dispassionate tones of the Victorian professional:

> **January 10th 1865. 6.45pm.** Captain Martin received intelligence by telegraph from Port Philip Heads, that Mr Harris, chief officer, the boat's crew and the lifeboat had arrived on board the ship 'John Bunyan' bound to this port, having been first picked up on Tuesday November 22nd by the whaling barque 'Henry Tabor' of New Bedford and transferred to the 'John Bunyan' on November 23rd.
> **11.30pm.** Mr Harris came on board.
> **January 11th. 7.30am.** The following came on board from the 'John Bunyan'. All well. John Clarke AB, Giovanni Ghotte AB, Richard Collins AB, Richard Cotter AB, James Rayner AB.

The captain's initial relief was soon tempered by the realisation that he had clearly made the wrong decision in abandoning the search for his men so soon. Nonetheless, he decided to tackle this head on and, on the morning

A mass of ships at Port Melbourne Pier. (Brodie Collection, La Trobe Picture Collection, State Library of Victoria)

of 11 January, as soon as his seamen were back on board, he wrote to the port authorities at Melbourne requesting an inquiry. Accordingly, the Government Shipping Master for Melbourne visited the *London* the same day, and conducted interviews with the crew. Interestingly, Robert Harris initially refused to speak to him, although he later gave a simple statement. Neither Harris, nor any of the survivors offered direct criticism of Captain Martin, although all of them noted that the *London* did not set lights or fire any rockets as it began to get dark to guide the boat's crew back to the ship.

Over the next two days, interviews with other members of the crew provoked more direct criticism. Or perhaps as much criticism as a man dared, bearing in mind that all of them needed good references from a captain to secure future employment. It's also notable that many of the desertions had already taken place by this time, and these were presumably the most disaffected men. Fred Diver, the second officer, defended his captain. However, James Chilvers, the boatswain, had witnessed Henry Darnford falling overboard – the incident that had started the whole chain of events. He was interviewed and stated that he never thought that the ship's boat had foundered and always believed the boat was safe. William Hosking, the quartermaster, agreed and added that 'the seamen did not consider that Captain Martin had acted right in going to sea during the night'. This opinion was supported by the third mate, and five seamen who were interviewed. The prevailing view was that the ship's boat was seaworthy, that the seas were not dangerous enough to swamp it, and that the captain should have stayed until the next morning while showing lights overnight. The ship's surgeon, Dr Faull, noted that Captain Martin asked some of the passengers whether he should remain any longer and was reassured that he had done all he could. However, the passengers were not professional seafarers. Two seamen even reported that Captain Martin had wanted to depart earlier than he did – in the middle of the afternoon – but was only prevented by some of the crew refusing his orders.

Interestingly, of the ten people named as being interviewed on the second and third days, five soon elected to leave the ship at Melbourne or simply deserted. However, none of the men who had been abandoned in the boat did so. They each worked on the *London* for its return trip to England, and chief officer Harris stayed on the ship for both its second voyage to Australia and its ill-fated final journey.

Three days after the final interview, on 16 January 1865, the Attorney General for Melbourne, George Higinbotham, delivered his verdict on Captain Martin:

> I am of opinion that the evidence taken by the shipping master does not furnish grounds for a charge of misdemeanour against the master of the *London*, under section 239 of the Merchant Shipping Act 1854 ... In view of all the circumstances, I think that a jury would have no hesitation in acquitting the master, on this evidence, of the serious charge of endangering the lives of his chief officer and men, and that he should not be subjected to the necessity of defending himself against such a charge.
> (*The Argus*, 17 Jan. 1865)

Caricature of George Higinbotham.

This must have been a source of considerable relief to Captain Martin. Having been exonerated, he now managed to recruit enough new crewmen to make up the deficit and readied the ship for sailing. Unfortunately for the captain, the return voyage did not begin well. On the scheduled day of departure, 4 February 1865, it was reported that seven men who were expected to join the ship had not done so and, soon after sailing, two of the new recruits who had claimed to be experienced seamen were deemed so incompetent that they were reduced in rank to the lowest possible grade.

The crew still seemed edgy and discontented, and incidents began to occur. Captain Martin made this entry in the log for 23 March 1865:

> On turning the crew to their usual work after dinner, it was found that Charles Harris, trimmer, was absent, and on Mr Diver, 2nd officer, calling him out of the forecastle about 13 minutes after everybody was at work, he became abusive. He was sent on the lower deck to wash paintwork, when he there became again so very abusive and insubordinate in language by calling Mr Diver 'a bloody nigger driver' etc. He was brought up before Mr Harris [chief officer] when he became so excitable as to bring a crowd of passengers around. He was sent below to Mr Harding, chief engineer, and work there given him.

Two days later, one of the stewards was found roaring drunk in a cabin belonging to a First Class passenger. He was sent to his berth, and it later transpired that he had stolen a bottle of whisky and two bottles of champagne, which later made him very sick. A week later, the unfortunate James Chilvers, the boatswain who had witnessed his crewmate falling overboard and who had implied criticism of his captain for not waiting longer to pick up the ship's boat, also got himself into trouble:

Mr Chilvers left the forecastle, came aft without being sent or called for, and commenced (before being spoken to) in a most abusive and insubordinate language saying he did not care about being on board the *London*, but that he could get a new ship or steamer when he arrived home. He was ordered off the quarterdeck by Captain Martin. He hesitated in leaving until ordered a second and third time, when he was at once sent to his cabin.

These flagrant breaches of discipline suggest that elements of the crew were still restless, and that the authority of the chain of command had been undermined. The most obvious cause for this was resentment that Captain Martin had been exonerated for abandoning his crewmen in the *London*'s boat, when this had clearly been the wrong course of action.

The ship's surgeon was also particularly busy attending to the passengers on the return trip, and two of them died on the voyage. No doubt, the captain was relieved when the *London* reached its home port at the end of April. The next voyage would be an opportunity to start again with a fresh crew, and there was still that target of the sixty-day passage to aim for.

The Second Voyage

There was a quick turnaround of only a few weeks while the *London* discharged her cargo, loaded a new one, and sought passengers and a crew for her second trip to Australia. Although it was usual for most of the crew to be discharged and then replaced with fresh personnel, the chain of command was typically left intact. However, when the ship set sail on 29 May 1865, no-one can have been surprised that Captain Martin had appointed a new boatswain, John Staden. There was a different second

Passengers boarding a ship.

officer, too – Arthur Ticehurst replaced the allegedly draconian Fred Diver. Robert Harris, of course, stayed on as chief officer.

Discipline among the crew was good, apart from a squabble involving Jeremiah McCarthy and three other seamen, who refused to go to work one day until they had been allowed to smoke their pipes. However, during the voyage there was an outbreak of smallpox. One crewman who had contracted the disease ashore passed it to three others. Fortunately, none of them died but the ship had to be put into quarantine on its arrival in Melbourne on 4 August. This marred a voyage that otherwise would have been a source of great satisfaction to Captain Martin because he had managed to complete the journey from Plymouth to Melbourne in sixty days. He had already met the target he had set for himself.

However, quarantine meant that no-one could go on shore until the medical authorities said so. After such a speedy outward voyage to Australia, the *London* anchored and just sat there in the waters off Melbourne, isolated. It must have been enormously vexing for everyone on board, and we can imagine Captain Martin and his officers patiently explaining what was happening to irritated passengers and crew alike, and hoping to diffuse tensions.

The whole ship was washed and fumigated, and everyone on board was monitored in case of any new episodes of smallpox. It was a frustrating time of inertia and, perhaps predictably, discipline soon started to break down again. When Mr Walker, one of the port's medical authorities, visited the ship to inspect it, Seaman Jeremiah McCarthy accosted him and to Captain Martin's utter dismay called him 'a damned son of a bitch'. The horrified captain attempted to intervene: 'On Captain Martin asking Jeremiah McCarthy to beg Mr Walker's pardon, he said he would be damned and buggered if he would; he became very abusive and [used] obscene language for some considerable time'. The next day someone broke into the chief officer's cabin and stole items. The day after this, a seaman refused to work: 'no bloody fear', he said when ordered to his duty. Fortunately, before such dissent could spread further, the quarantine ended on the fourth day, but this triggered some heavy drinking with no less than eleven crewmen noted in the log as reprimanded for getting drunk, and there were multiple episodes of being absent without leave. There were desertions, too – eighteen of them. The notorious Jeremiah McCarthy became repeatedly so drunk that he was unable to work for several days on end. Captain Martin must have hoped that he would desert; but he did not oblige.

The passengers were allowed to leave as long as they would consent to being vaccinated against smallpox. One couple refused and were sent ashore to resume quarantine until such time as the authorities could be assured they were not ill, but the rest were allowed to depart.

The SS *London* set sail back to England in September 1865 and, apart from some minor breaches of discipline, the captain for once had a relatively straightforward voyage home.

Once back in the capital, the efficient turnaround of the ship was repeated ready for the SS *London*'s third and final voyage. Captain Martin may well have prayed for an uneventful voyage and a trouble-free crew.

Medical supervision by a doctor, looking for any signs of infection as passengers leave ship.

4
The Crew

The life afloat for crews of Victorian merchant ships was insecure. Employment was unpredictable; officers could be strict; there were significant risks; and they were often taken away from their families for long periods.

There were ninety-two members of the crew on the SS *London*'s final voyage, and they are identified in Appendix 1. The oldest employee was the captain, John Bohun Martin, at forty-eight years of age, while the youngest was fourteen-year-old ship's boy, Alfred White, who was one of the few who would survive the disaster.

In terms of basic functions, the crew's roles can be summarised as follows:

Seamen	42
Deck officers	7
Engineering and mechanical	16
Stewards and servants	13
Catering	6
Other specialists	8

While the seamen were the biggest single group of employees, the other workers on the ship collectively amounted to more than half the crew. People often moved from catering, servant or technical posts ashore to similar careers afloat quite easily, and there were nine men on the *London* who were going to sea for the first time. The career paths, experiences, and responsibilities of the various crewmembers differed markedly.

Seamen

Many seamen in the nineteenth century began their careers as ship's boys, typically joining their first vessel in their early teens with little or no significant seafaring experience. They initially performed lowly, unskilled tasks such as cleaning, serving the crew's food, and assisting other personnel as requested, but they gradually picked up seafaring skills on the job and were eventually able to take on the role of a fully fledged seaman when they were deemed to have sufficient experience. The *London* had two ship's boys: sixteen-year-old Edward Logan, and fourteen-year-old Alfred White.

Seamen could also undertake an official apprenticeship, beginning with formal tuition in an approved training school before going to sea to complete their education. In fact, a number of charities such as the Marine Society saw seafaring training and apprenticeships as a means to instil discipline and a sense of purpose into the lives of vulnerable youths trapped in a life of poverty or neglect. There were even state-sponsored schools that sought to provide safety and a future career for homeless, orphaned, and destitute boys, such as the training ship *Grampian* in Belfast. Other institutions were created explicitly to reform young men who exhibited antisocial behaviour by exposing them to a highly disciplined environment. These 'reformatory boys' were accommodated in facilities such as the training ship *Akbar* in Liverpool. As a result many young boys were taken off the streets, from homes or workhouses where they were neglected, or from organisations that dealt with juvenile criminals, and enlisted for an apprenticeship. Some of these later found employment in the Royal Navy and some in the merchant service.

After their years of teenage instruction as boy or apprentice, the next rung on the seaman's career ladder was the position of ordinary seaman or simply 'seaman'. This role still had a significant element of training attached to it, and thus these men were always under the supervision of more experienced personnel from whom they 'learned the ropes'. Most ordinary seamen were aged in their late teens or early twenties.

Above left: Alfred White, ship's boy, was only fourteen.

Above right: A Victorian ship's boy in his seagoing jersey and cap.

Once he had developed sufficient skills, a man could move up the seaman's hierarchy to the position of able seaman. A man of this rank could, by tradition, 'hand, reef, and steer'. In other words he had sufficient knowledge to understand and work all the ship's ropes ('hand'), he could take in and secure the ship's sails even in heavy weather ('reef'), and he could operate the ship's wheel and follow navigational instructions ('steer'). The role of able seaman allowed significantly greater responsibility, and demanded physical fitness. Racing aloft to attend to sails required bravery and agility, especially in rough weather and, despite the use of blocks and pulleys, a man needed to be strong to haul on the ship's ropes many times throughout the day. It is small wonder that one of the commonest medical problems faced by Victorian seamen was that of the hernia.

The thirty-five able seamen on board the *London* for its last voyage ranged from nineteen-year-old James Gough, who was about as young as an able seaman could be, to Andrew Anderson, who was forty-one. The average age was mid-twenties – so the crew was dominated by young men, fit and strong. Most of the seamen were British, but there were fifteen other Europeans – one Dutchman, five Germans, and nine Scandinavians – from seafaring nations that frequently contributed to the crews of British ships.

An individual might remain an able seaman for the rest of his career but there was hope of advancement for men with the right ability, most notably to the post of boatswain (or 'bosun'), who was rated as the most senior seaman on board. His role was to enforce discipline and to organise the men who worked the ship. Essentially he had to ensure that the day's work was done safely, properly, and in a timely manner, and that officers were obeyed. On the *London* the boatswain was John Staden, who at thirty-four years of age would have been considered a very experienced hand. His deputy, Daniel Smith, took on Staden's role when he was off duty, and was known as the boatswain's mate.

Able seaman at the wheel.

The day-to-day duties of seamen became quite monotonous when on a prolonged voyage at sea in fair weather. Elements permitting, the day began with scrubbing of the ship's decks – a tradition that was rooted in the Royal Navy's concept of an orderly ship, coupled with the notion that cleanliness helped to prevent disease. During the day, seamen responded to the ship-handling and navigational orders of the officer in charge of the main deck, which could, for example, require them to reef or loose individual sails, haul on ropes to reposition yards, or take a turn at the wheel. Seamen might be asked to perform a variety of other duties at an officer's discretion – rearranging or loading cargo, painting the ship, polishing the brass, helping with repairs, retrieving stores or other items from the hold, teaching more junior crewmates, entertaining the passengers and so forth. Seamen were also posted as lookouts to survey the way ahead for wrecks, deteriorating weather, or other threats. At night, men were allocated to keeping watch on deck for similar reasons.

William Caius Crutchley served on the Blackwall frigate *Essex* in the 1860s, which belonged to the Wigrams. He recalled that in fine weather the seamen were not expected to work too hard:

> Soon after taking up our quarters on board, we had our first lesson in 'Blackwall fashion'. Davies and I were on a stage on the ship's side *busily* painting when one of the Jacks put his head over: 'Here, you chaps, you're doing too much work, that ain't Blackwall fashion,' and I must confess that we immediately complied with the regulation.
>
> I was a maintop man, and, being under the immediate eye of the officer of the watch, had not that same freedom of action they enjoyed forward, and yet I seem to remember some association between the game of euchre [a card game] and the maintop on fine afternoons.

By the 1860s, conventional twelve-hour clocks or chronometers were used on board British ships, but there was another way in which the passage of

Seamen loading livestock for the voyage.

time was recorded, following a pattern established by the Royal Navy. Each day was divided into seven 'watch periods' per twenty-four hours, which allowed seamen and officers to be allotted specific four-to-eight hour time periods for being on duty. These were:

Afternoon watch	Noon to 4.00 p.m.
First dogwatch	4.00 p.m. to 6.00 p.m.
Second dogwatch	6.00 p.m. to 8.00 p.m.
First night watch	8.00 p.m. to midnight
Middle or mid watch	Midnight to 4.00 a.m.
Morning watch	4.00 to 8.00 a.m.
Forenoon watch	8.00 a.m. to noon.

During each of these watches, a bell was rung every half an hour to provide an audible indication of the passage of time. So, for example, the bell would be rung three times after one-and-a-half hours of the morning watch and eight times to indicate its conclusion. This was important because few men carried a time-piece and yet each had to know when to be at their agreed station. New crewmen and passengers alike rapidly learned how to interpret this frequent bell ringing.

Personal possessions were stored in a seaman's trunk, although important items such as money or a pipe were often kept about the person. In terms of dress, it is most likely that seamen on the *London* wore no uniform, and some of them might still have gone barefoot. By the mid-1860s, some shipping lines had introduced jerseys carrying the name of the company or its flag, and ribbons to tie around seaman's caps with the name of the ship or the shipping line. However, most companies did not provide uniforms, so seamen often wore their own clothing.

By the 1860s some seamen wore a company jersey and cap.

Deck Officers

The deck officers were headed by the captain, known officially as the ship's master. On the *London* this position was held by John Bohun Martin. The captain and his officers were responsible for the navigation and working of the ship, the safety of everyone on board, the discipline of the crew, and the transportation of the vessel's cargo. Captain Martin's immediate deputy was the first mate, Robert Harris, followed by the second mate, Arthur Ticehurst, then third mate, Arthur Angel. These job titles were beginning to change at this time and the alternative terms 'chief officer', 'second officer', and so forth were used interchangeably with the traditional name of 'mate'.

The officers of the *London* were a fairly middle-class set, as might perhaps be expected on a ship that prided itself on the luxury and service that it afforded to its passengers. For example, Second Officer Arthur Ticehurst's father was a surgeon who became Mayor of Hastings, and Arthur Angel's father was a professor of music and the organist at Exeter Cathedral. A ship's officers were expected to be able to interact with the passengers in a polite and comfortable manner, and so their social background was important to employers.

In 1865, it was a legal requirement that men could not be ranked above the level of third officer unless they were in possession of a mate's certificate. This requirement had been introduced by law in 1850 for mates working on foreign-going ships. Prospective candidates had to sit an examination, usually at their own expense. Arthur Angel, for example, the *London*'s third officer, sat his examinations to become a second officer in the Port of London in January 1865. This cost him £1, and he was successful. He was granted a second mate's certificate, and it was then only a matter of time before Arthur had to decide that he had enough practical experience on

A ship's mate in the mid-1860s; the *London*'s officers probably wore a long frock coat and cap like this.

top of his qualification to apply for positions as second mate on another ship. There was another examination for men who wished to become first officers, and yet a third different exam for those who sought to become a ship's captain or 'master'. When the requirement to become certificated was introduced in 1850, men who were already operating at the required level, or who thought they should be, were allowed to apply for a certificate based on their previous experience. These men, if successful, thus avoided having to sit the new examination. Robert Harris, the ship's chief officer, earned his second mate's certificate in this manner, having by 1851 served ten years as apprentice and mate on various ships; however, he had to sit an exam for his first mate's certificate.

Young men who aspired to become officers in the merchant service generally had three routes in. The first was to take up an apprenticeship: a shore-based course was followed by a three-year apprenticeship at sea under a designated officer. These officer apprentices were commonly termed cadets, to distinguish them from apprentice seamen. The second route was to rise through the ranks from humble seaman, but this became progressively harder to do as the nineteenth century advanced, because shipowners wanted to identify suitable officer material themselves at an early age.

However, certain prestigious shipping lines like Wigram & Sons offered a third route to officer status. Parents or guardians could pay for their son to be appointed as a midshipman, and to be trained while they worked. On the *London*, there were two midshipmen or 'middies' – Walter Edwards and Robert Clough. Once they had completed their training they could be appointed as fourth officer or third officer but, as noted above, they needed to sit an examination to progress further.

There are no illustrations of officers from the *London* in uniform, but they probably would have worn blue frock coats and matching trousers. Initially, Money Wigram & Sons' officers wore the lion and crown emblem of the old East India Company on their caps, but this gradually gave way

This apprentice officer worked for George Smith & Sons and has the company flag on his cap badge.

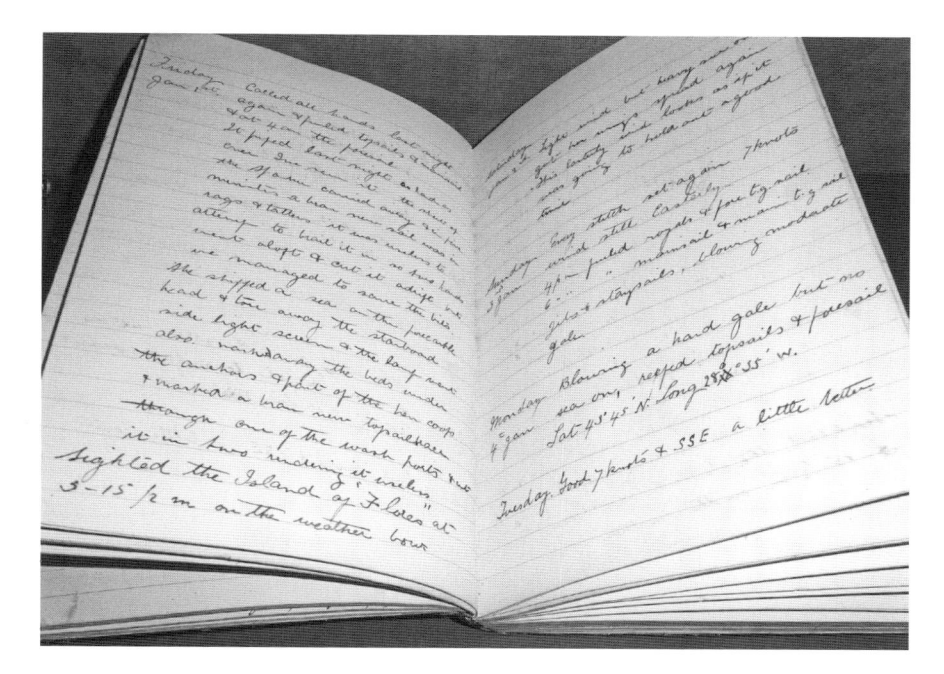

Above: Trainee and junior officers were encouraged to keep their own logs of the voyage as part of their training.

Right: A midshipman in 1866.

to the Wigram company flag instead, and their frock coats had gilt buttons bearing the flag as well. Many shipping lines at this time did not have uniforms, but the more upmarket passenger-carrying companies such as P&O were early adopters, and Money Wigram & Sons would have seen themselves in this prestige bracket.

Unlike seamen, the officers on a passenger ship would generally have had a cabin to themselves, although cadets and junior officers often shared. The captain had a large cabin, which included a small dining area for receiving guests. Other officers had much smaller cabins, but with a bunk-like bed at their disposal, rather than the hammocks used by seamen.

Above left: A ship's officer for P&O in the 1860s.

Above right: An officer's button from a Money Wigram & Sons' uniform, showing the company flag crossed with an anchor.

Engineering Personnel

Engineers became indispensable as soon as the marine steam engine was developed. These officers managed the ship's engines and had responsibility for other mechanical devices on board such as pumps and winches. The welfare of the ship, crew, passengers and cargo depended on the engines functioning properly and, as a result, the Board of Trade instigated a method for certificating marine engineers in 1861, not long after introducing a similar requirement for ships' captains and mates.

The most senior officer was usually termed the chief or first engineer; on the SS *London*, this role was undertaken by thirty-six-year-old Cornishman, John Jones. Like many men who filled these positions at this time, Jones had been an engineer ashore before pursuing a maritime career. No prior experience of seafaring was required initially – it was the technical knowledge of engines that mattered. Consequently, unlike the ship's deck officers, who usually had a maritime career stretching back until their early teens, marine engineering officers at this time often did not take up seagoing careers until later in life.

The chief engineer was accompanied on the *London* by a second engineer, John Greenhill, and a third engineer, John Armour. These engineering officers were responsible for the men working in the engine room, who consisted of two types in the 1860s: firemen and trimmers. Firemen were equivalent to stokers in the Royal Navy: they shovelled the coal into the furnaces on board the *London* that powered the vessel's steam engines. The *London* carried seven firemen, with one of them, John Morley, designated as leading firemen. This allowed firemen to work in pairs for up to eight hours per day. In addition, the storekeeper, Henry Jenkins, was allowed to work as a fireman when his other duties permitted.

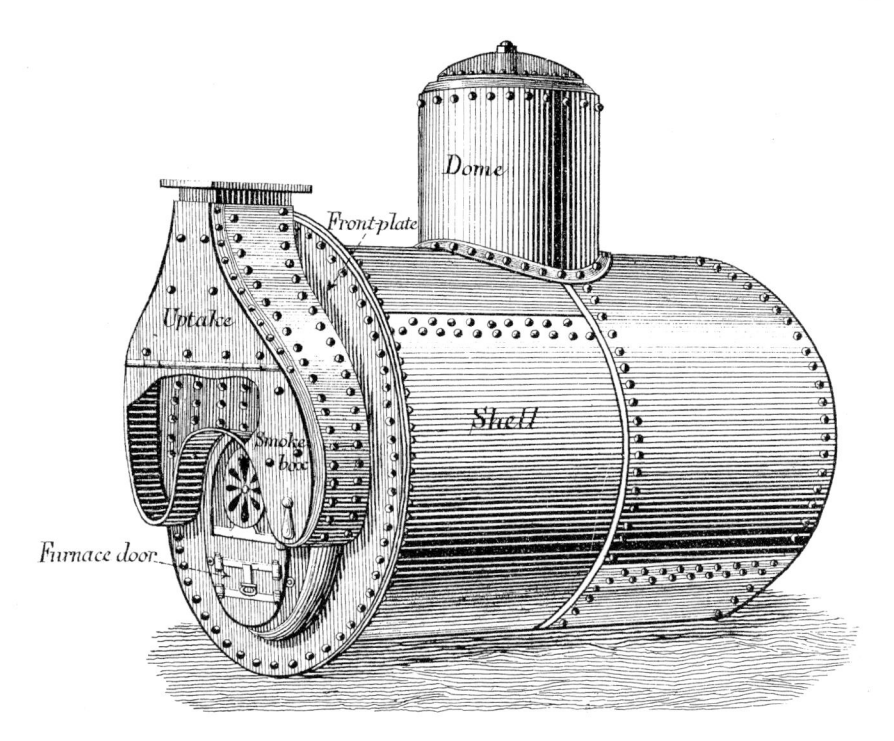

Boiler of ship's engine showing furnace where firemen stoked the coal.

The job of the trimmer was to manage the ship's coal stocks. He ensured that the firemen always had sufficient coal available, and cleared away ash from the furnaces to ensure the burning was efficient. The huge amounts of coal carried by steamships constituted a considerable weight; it was vital for trimmers to manage the ship's coal stocks so that they were run down evenly in storage areas, otherwise the imbalance caused by an uneven load could allow the ship to 'lose its trim', hence the name for this role. The *London* carried three trimmers.

The role of fireman and trimmer was hot, dirty, noisy, and physically demanding. These men were not expected to wear a uniform, and usually worked in loose overalls. They were never seen by passengers unless the chief engineer organised a tour of the engine room for selected guests.

There were also two winch operators on the ship who reported to the engineering officers. Winches had a variety of functions but were, for example, important for moving heavy items.

Other Crewmembers

Passenger ships carried a range of personnel other than seamen, deck officers, and engine-room staff. These employees were recruited according to the same terms and conditions as everyone else, but had skills or experience unrelated to the handling of the ship and its engines.

All food on board the *London* was prepared by the vessel's catering personnel, headed by the ship's cook, Henry Appleton. He must have been a very busy man, given the large number of passengers and crew he had to support – particularly since his own team was remarkably small, consisting only of a sculleryman, butcher, baker, and storekeeper.

On board the *London* were a range of stewards and servants. Their roles were to attend First Class passengers in their cabins – providing fresh linen, making beds, sweeping rooms, and supplying water with which to wash. They provided very limited cabin services to other classes of passengers, who were expected to be self-sufficient. Stewards assisted the cook by serving food at meal times, and may have assisted with food preparation; they also provided hot and cold drinks for passengers when requested. The stewards were the passengers' attendants and on prestigious vessels such as the *London* would have been dressed like footmen in a large country house. Captain Martin had his own steward, John Huckstepp, and his own cook, the appropriately named Thomas Ham.

A particularly important person on board the *London* was the ship's doctor, known for historical reasons as its surgeon. This role was a medical 'jack of all trades', who might need to deal with everything from seasickness and insomnia among the passengers to serious accidents and contagious diseases. The long journey to Australia meant that passengers were keen to know that they had access to medical assistance if required. The provision of a surgeon was, in fact, a legal requirement, but promotional materials for the *London* stress the fact that the ship 'will carry an experienced surgeon'. Mr John Vivian Faull MRCS LSA was the surgeon employed by Money Wigram & Sons on the *London*, and he had been working for the company since 1864. On the face of it, he was not perhaps the most qualified person for the role. His previous appointment had been to manage the 'female section' of the Middlesex County Lunatic Asylum, and he was qualified as a surgeon

Part of the kitchen or galley on a Victorian ship.

Clergyman in the saloon conducting Sunday worship.

(MRCS) and apothecary (LSA). However, the role of ship's surgeon was not particularly popular within the medical professions because it required long periods of time away from home, and was not well paid. In addition, the position of ship's surgeon was widely regarded by shore-based doctors as the intellectual and professional 'poor relation' of other areas of practice. However, beggars could not be choosers; the ship had to have a surgeon and shipping lines took whoever they could get. It was not a falsehood for Money Wigram & Sons to describe Mr Faull as an 'experienced' surgeon: at thirty-seven years of age, and having been qualified for over ten years, he was 'experienced'. Yet, his previous professional practice on appointment was not especially relevant.

The *London* also carried a purser, responsible for a myriad of administrative tasks related to the ship's paperwork and finances, a carpenter who conducted running repairs of the ship as necessary, and a sailmaker.

Commercial ships generally did not carry a clergyman on the crew, although it was common for the captain to invite any minister travelling with the passengers to conduct 'divine worship' on a Sunday. The *London* was actually carrying three ministers among its passengers. In the absence of a clergyman, the captain himself might lead the weekly Christian service if he was of a religious inclination. However, despite our modern-day perception of Victorians as devout and zealous Christians, many captains were not inclined to take this responsibility.

Women Crewmembers

A notable feature of the *London*'s list of crewmembers is that there is only one woman among them. In the nineteenth century, women were not employed in seagoing roles except in the merchant service, where minor inroads were gradually being made.

Twenty-two-year-old Grace Logan is listed as the *London*'s only stewardess. Women began to occasionally feature as crewmembers on merchant ships in the early Victorian era, usually performing domestic duties. The existence of one or two women on board a ship among an overwhelming majority of male crewmen raised a few Victorian eyebrows, particularly since there was a high level of cynicism regarding the moral conduct of seamen. So a woman who chose to enter into this environment could be viewed with some suspicion.

Grace Logan's role as stewardess was principally to attend to the needs of female passengers and children. To some extent she was both nurse and ladies' maid. She would have tended children and women if they were ill, and assisted them with their dress, bedding, and food. However, many wealthy passengers in this era took their own servants to sea with them. Elizabeth Hartley, for example, was a servant employed by First Class passengers James and Sarah Thomas, who were travelling with their two children. Elizabeth attended to the Thomas family according to their needs, and accompanied them as they directed, although she slept in a separate cabin in Third Class.

In the 1860s, it was unthinkable that a woman could perform any other role on a ship – and certainly not serve as a seaman, officer, engineer, or even a cook. However, later in the nineteenth century, as ships became larger and passenger demands greater, women did begin to take on a wider range of domestic roles at sea such as laundress, hairdresser, waitress, and nurse.

Conditions of Service

Throughout the nineteenth century the men – and the few women – who worked on merchant ships were employed for one voyage at a time. From 1845 onwards, they 'signed up' at the beginning of each foreign voyage and were discharged at its conclusion. Even worse, if the vessel was damaged and needed immediate repairs, sank, or was taken out of service for any other reason, then the whole crew was instantly dismissed without further pay. It was a shipowner's world and crewmembers had little security of employment.

There was often an understanding that an owner would continue to employ a particular captain and senior officers if they were competent,

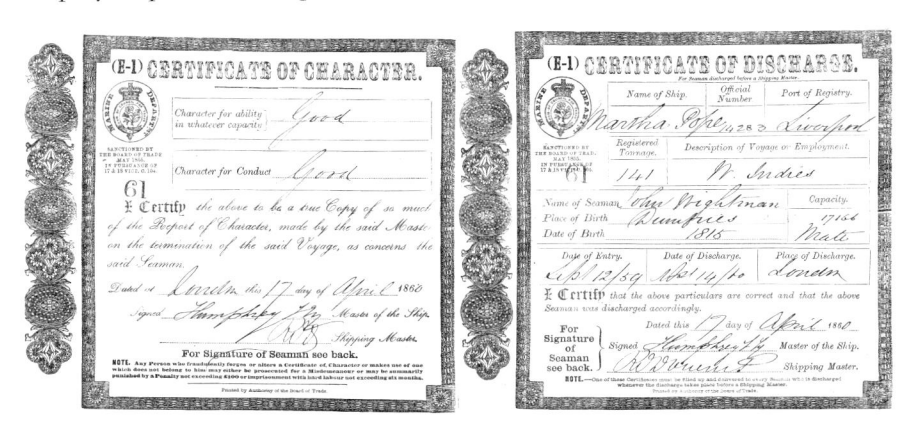

A certificate of character and discharge acted like an employment reference for Victorian seamen.

and Money Wigram & Sons operated this arrangement. The *London*'s four senior deck officers had all served on its two previous voyages. The two midshipmen were new to the *London*, with one of them embarking on his first-ever voyage. However, employment security was much more tenuous for other members of the crew. A vessel might take several weeks to prepare for the next voyage, during which time the crewmen from the previous voyage would generally be discharged so that the shipping line did not have to pay them. After completing each voyage, crewmembers were given a discharge certificate, which acted like an employer's reference. This took various forms, but it recorded the person's ability (professional skills) and conduct (timeliness, sobriety, attitude). These pieces of paper helped crewmen find another ship, but for many seamen their lives were one long round of ship chasing. A few personnel were retained from previous voyages of the *London* when it departed on its final sailing: John Staden, the boatswain, was a valuable asset and re-engaged, as were some of the other senior specialist personnel such as the surgeon, cook, baker and butcher; one of the ship's boys was part-way through his training and was retained; and several fireman were allowed to re-enlist. All in all, twenty-nine of the ninety-two crew are known to have served on the *London*'s previous voyage, but most of the seamen had not.

When they were employed on board the *London* its personnel all signed a crew agreement where they were generally exhorted to 'conduct themselves in an orderly, faithful, sober and honest manner and to be at all times diligent in their respective duties'. Here, the ship's owners were obliged to state the rate of pay, the food they would provide, and the penalties for disciplinary breaches. The crew agreement applied to every employee on board, including the captain, and so everyone had to sign it. The agreement usually specified the types of conduct that would not be tolerated and they typically included: striking or assaulting anyone on board; desertion; drunkenness; wilful disobedience of lawful commands; insolent or contemptuous language; absence without leave; theft or damage of cargo; and neglect of duty (e.g., sleeping while on duty). Some employers also specified other offences, such as 'behaving inappropriately on Sunday'.

There was a particular attention to the need for sobriety on the part of the crew and formal written references for officers tended to reinforce this. Phrases such as 'a sober, faithful and competent officer' were widely used. This emphasis did reflect Victorian society's horror of alcoholic excess, but there was also the practical consideration that drunkenness on a ship could endanger lives or even the whole vessel. A drunken man might not keep watch properly and fail to detect danger until it was too late; he might pursue the wrong navigational course at the wheel; he might fall from the rigging; he might assault others, and so forth.

The main method of dealing with breaches in discipline was to enforce the payment of fines, by docking the pay of crewmembers at the conclusion of a voyage. But a captain could take other approaches. These might include forcing a crewman to undertake menial duties such as cleaning, confining him somewhere on board, or 'disrating' an employee, which meant forcing an instant lowering of rank (and pay). In extreme cases a captain could order a crewman's formal arrest.

However, discipline in the merchant service was more relaxed than, say, the Royal Navy. William Crutchley, an able seaman on a Wigram ship in the 1860s, recalled the crew's approach to a third mate who worked them too hard:

> There was one night the third mate had already given rather more trouble than we thought he ought to have done, when he put the finishing touch by giving the order to set a lower studding-sail. The night was pitch dark, and we were being as awkward and as slow as we knew how to be. The captain was on deck, and ordered the third to go forward and see what the delay was caused by. He did so promptly, and got a ball of spun yarn thrown at his head by a hand unknown, on which he retired aft and told the skipper. Now Captain Attwood was a man who feared nothing or no one, and he promptly came to inquire who had 'thrown a ball of spun yarn at his third mate's head?' Such was the temper of the men that the betting was very even as to what he was likely to get himself; but after some talk of more or less lurid hue, Davies solved the difficulty by saying, 'Look here, Captain Attwood, if you want the work done we can do it, but we are not going to be humbugged round by that third mate of yours; now we'll show you how to set a stunsail'.

There was further potential sanction for ships' officers. From 1855, the government's Registrar General of Shipping and Seamen kept a permanent record of officers who had perpetrated offences that required formal disciplinary action on board ship, such as drunkenness, violence, negligence and theft. The registrar's so-called 'Black Books' also described serious crimes committed ashore. If found guilty, an offender could have his mate's or master's certificate rescinded – either permanently or for a specified duration – which effectively prevented the officer from working at sea, since his certificates had to be shown to prospective employers.

Given the lack of confidence that shipowners placed in the long-term employment of their seamen beyond a single voyage, and the sometimes harsh conditions of employment, it is not surprising that crewmembers could display a lack of loyalty. Desertion or 'jumping ship' at a convenient port meant that a seaman forfeited his wages earned for the voyage thus far, but it was a speedy means to escape a boring cruise, a cruel officer, poor pay, or stingy rations. Some men left a ship simply because they wanted a more exotic final destination and hoped to use their careers to explore the world. Just before the SS *London* left Gravesend, six seamen abandoned the ship, hoping to find better prospects elsewhere. Their reasons for leaving will remain forever a mystery, but on later discovering the *London*'s fate these men must have been enormously thankful that they had chosen not to stay on board. At the same time, one wonders at the state of mind of the four seamen recruited to replace these deserters at Plymouth once they could see that the *London* was going to founder. Edward Thomas, Charles Ansell,

John Mulloney, and Robert Stephens must have cursed their luck when they realised they were doomed. None of them survived.

Risks on Board

The most notable danger to crewmembers was shipwreck. Vessels were lost with depressing frequency, and Victorian newspapers are crammed with examples. Ships were battered by storms, got lost in the fog, caught fire, collided with other vessels, and suffered from construction defects. For the period from 1867 to 1871, British Board of Trade figures reveal 7,062 shipping 'casualties', being events in which a vessel was at least seriously damaged. In these incidents, a total of 2,598 ships were lost, and 8,807 crewmembers and passengers died. This equates to an alarming thirty-four deaths at sea *every week*. And yet these figures refer only to the coast of Britain and say nothing of the many British vessels lost mid-Atlantic, or in the Baltic, the Indian Ocean, Australian waters and so forth.

A good example of the personal effects of shipwreck is afforded by the career history of able seaman John King on the *London*. He was only twenty-eight years of age and yet the *London* became his third wreck in five years. In December 1861, King was on the crew of the *Alma,* which was caught in a sudden violent storm off the shore of Australia while discharging ballast. The strain on the ship's anchor cable proved too much and it snapped, sending the vessel hurtling onto the coastal rocks. The local lifeboatmen managed to get a line on board, and each crewmember from the *Alma* worked his way precariously along this rope, hand over hand, above the raging seas and sharp rocks to reach safety. Eventually all twenty-four crewmen made it ashore, but they were very fortunate to survive: the *Alma* was soon smashed into thousands of pieces and scattered over 10 miles of beach.

Wreck of the *Duncan Dunbar.* (Brodie Collection, La Trobe Picture Collection, State Library of Victoria)

John King's second shipwreck was while serving on the *Duncan Dunbar*, a dramatic incident that received much news coverage at the time. This passenger ship ran aground on a reef off the coast of Brazil on the night of 7 October 1865. At daybreak, the crew managed to take the terrified passengers off the ship by lowering them over the stern in a chair, one at a time. They were transferred via the ship's boat to a small islet covered with weed and vermin. In temperatures of 44°C, 117 people hoped to survive until they might sight a passing ship. They managed to retrieve food and water from the *Duncan Dunbar* and erected a tent for shelter using the ship's sails. The captain took some of the crew in the ship's boat and made for Pernambuco, and arranged for a steamship to return and rescue his crew and passengers ten days later.

The unfortunate John King survived this second dreadful experience and returned to England just in time to join the crew of the SS *London*. By coincidence, at least one of the passengers on board the SS *London* was also a survivor of the *Duncan Dunbar*.

Seamen were exposed to other risks, quite apart from the danger of shipwreck. This included falls from the rigging. Sometimes a man who lost his footing fell to the deck, which commonly resulted in loss of life, but even the 'soft' landing of a fall into the sea frequently led to the victim's death. It is a sad fact that most Victorian seamen could not swim, and even those that did manage to stay alive were not guaranteed survival. The freezing waters of the north Atlantic in winter, for example, would kill a man in minutes, and the long time required for a ship to slow down and turn to pick him up meant that he usually was never seen again.

Employment at sea came with its own set of diseases as well. Fortunately, many of these were on the wane by the mid-1860s. The 1840s had seen a very dramatic rise in the incidence of 'ship fever' (a form of typhus) among crowded emigrant ships, but twenty years later this was much less prevalent. Scurvy was still occasionally encountered because of the restricted diet that many seamen were subject to, and shipowners such as Wigrams were obliged to provide their crews with regular supplements of

Administration of regular doses of lime juice helped Victorian seamen eliminate the risk of scurvy.

lime juice to prevent it. As sanitation and the ability to provide clean water progressed on land and at sea, diseases such as dysentery and cholera, which only decades before had killed thousands of seamen, also became much less common in Europe. However, there were still risks of infection. Notable examples include venereal disease, often contracted from sexual intercourse with prostitutes in busy ports, and tropical infections such as malaria and yellow fever, which were common on the coast of Africa and South America.

Seamen and Society

Victorian society viewed seamen as morally suspect. They were stereotyped as loose-living men with a cavalier attitude to the twin contemporary evils of alcohol and sex. In December 1865, the month that the SS *London* set sail on her last voyage, Captain Thomas Stuart wrote that sailors were too often men without a high sense of morality because they were 'subject to temptations to which the peculiar circumstances of their position, in a marked degree, expose them; and hitherto little care has been taken to guard them against the consequences of such exposure.'

In his book *The History of Drink*, published in 1878, James Samuelson protested that it was seafaring men who were largely responsible for public drunkenness. The main problem, he revealed, was the men of the lower socioeconomic groups, especially 'the vicious classes in the great seaports'. These seamen 'whose chief employment is drinking' were the group in society responsible for England's 'unenviable reputation for drunkenness among the nations of the world'.

Seamen were renowned too for their gambling, their frequent use of bad language or 'nautical oaths', and their inattention to regular Christian worship. Whole religious societies arose to attend specifically to the moral conduct of seamen. These included the Marine Temperance Society, the Society for the Promotion of Missions to Seamen, the Wesleyan Seamen's Mission, the Sailors and Soldiers Temperance Union, and many more.

Once removed from the 'civilising' influence of land-based society and the Church, some feared that passengers and crew alike would indulge in immoral behaviour: drinking, gambling, lewdness, and romance. P&O even felt obliged during this era to issue written instructions to their officers not to engage in romantic liaisons with female passengers. So it is no surprise that travellers could approach a voyage with a certain amount of trepidation. The Reverend William Neville took a voyage to Africa in 1858 and was pleasantly surprised not to find the 'den of iniquity' he had been led to expect:

> The Captain is a Scotchman and from his demeanour and conversation I am of opinion he would not permit any breach of decorum on the part of any passenger to pass unnoticed. But as yet, happily, I have witnessed nothing of the kind, nor experienced any of that unpleasantness which I was forewarned at Plymouth to be prepared to encounter.

Port of London Society,
FOR
PROMOTING RELIGION AMONG SEAMEN.

On TUESDAY, FEBRUARY 13, 1821,
A PUBLIC MEETING OF LADIES & GENTLEMEN,
WHO
Feel an Interest in the Religious Instruction of Seamen,
WILL BE HELD
AT FREEMASONS' HALL, GREAT QUEEN-STREET,
Lincoln's Inn Fields.

THE RIGHT HONORABLE J. C. VILLIERS, M. P.
WILL TAKE THE CHAIR AT TWELVE O'CLOCK PRECISELY.

This Ticket will admit the Bearer and his Friends.

THE ABOVE REPRESENTS THE INTERIOR OF THE FLOATING CHAPEL.

The moral character of seamen was subject to considerable attention by Christians in the nineteenth century.

The London City Mission were so concerned about the moral conduct of seamen that they appointed missionaries to tend to their spiritual needs. One of these evangelists was allocated to the East India Docks, from which the SS *London* departed on its last voyage, and his observations from 1866 were published in an article:

> The longer I am engaged in missionary work in the docks, the more am I impressed with the amount of wickedness abounding among seamen. The iniquity which for nearly two years I witnessed in my former district, known as St. Giles's, was nothing when compared with the open profligacy and confirmed drunkenness which is to be found among sailors ... Our 'British tars' far exceed their foreign brethren in brutality and vice. It is really lamentable to see the number of our English seamen who live more like the beasts that perish, than men possessing immortal souls, and what is a disgrace to our country may be seen in our docks at all times when a ship is leaving for some foreign port, in the fact that our seamen seem as if they could not face the winds and the waves, nor take farewell of their native shore, but in a state of intoxication. The brave and noble captain of the ill-fated ship *London*, said to me before leaving the docks on his last voyage, 'It is a great pity we cannot get our sailors to leave our ports in a sober state'.
> (*London City Mission Magazine*, 1 Aug. 1866)

Interestingly, in the same article, the missionary goes on to explain that he visited the SS *London* on the day of her departure, 28 December 1865:

> I remember having a conversation with the chief mate [Robert Harris], who ... expressed to me his regret that a seafaring life was so detrimental to a Christian's spiritual prosperity, and yet, perhaps, there was no profession in which implicit confidence in God was more necessary. As for the Captain, I always found him exceedingly kind and helpful to me in my work. In his manner I always found him slow to speak, and never making an ostentatious display of his religion, but calmly and earnestly serving God in that position where He had placed him.
>
> One might surely have thought that the loss of this ship, with 200 souls, would have proved a solemn warning to seamen generally, and especially to those of her crew who were saved from a watery grave; but facts show that this was not the case, for I have seen and conversed with two of the crew who escaped, and they informed me, by way of boasting, that as soon as they reached London both of them took the first opportunity of getting drunk – I suppose to express their gratitude for their miraculous deliverance.

5

The Captain

Captain John Bohun Martin was master of the SS *London* for its first two voyages as well as the ship's tragic final voyage. It is important to understand him and his approach to command, since the fate of the entire ship and its occupants depended upon his leadership, and a number of his actions have been called into question.

John Martin was born at Brompton, London, on 27 April 1819. His father, Edward, was an 'upholder' – he ran a shop selling and repairing household wares. The business did well: Edward employed three assistants to work with him, including one of his own sons, and he could also afford a family servant. His wife, Elizabeth, did not need to pursue paid employment and managed their home. John Martin, however, decided from a young age that the life of a shopkeeper was not for him and that he wanted to go to sea. He was probably at least partly motivated by the fact that, since he was not the oldest son, he knew he would not inherit much from his father, and certainly not the family business or home. He would have to make his own way in life.

Captain John Bohun Martin.

John Martin's Career

Some of the original records related to John Martin's employment are missing, but from various sources his seagoing career can be pieced together. In about 1836, the teenage Martin was appointed as midshipman, or 'trainee officer', on board the Wigram & Green ship *True Briton*. He had no prior seagoing experience at all, but this did not matter. A father with the right connections *paid* for his son to become a midshipman on a Blackwall frigate because it was considered such a fine opening in life with excellent prospects. All training was then given on the job. John Martin's father, Edward, would have been charged about £50 per voyage for the privilege of his son's maritime education. In addition, he would have purchased his son's uniform, and provided him with mess money (for food) and pocket money (for leisure). After maybe three or four voyages the parental charges were dropped and the midshipman began to earn a small wage.

His family's middle-class status would have helped John Martin secure this potentially lucrative appointment. Shipping lines such as Wigram & Green, with an eye on the richer end of the passenger market, were keen to employ educated young men of good character. Besides, ships such as the *True Briton* were the lineal descendants of the East Indiamen and their owners were determined to emulate the traditions of the old company – in particular that they be commanded and officered by men who were gentlemen trained as expert seamen.

The investment in this young man's early career certainly paid off, because John Martin proved to be a reliable officer and was retained by the ship's owners for his entire career.

The *True Briton* was a three-masted sailing ship built by Wigram & Green at their Blackwall yards, but it was built by the Wigram side of the business and thus was run by the Wigrams. It was a comparatively small ship at just under 650 tons, with a crew of around fifty.

John Martin's appointment to the *True Briton* lasted four years, during which time he served initially under Captain Foord, but then for the most part under the well-known and highly respected Captain Charles Beach. The *True Briton* carried about ninety passengers, but also transported cargo, and sailed regularly to India. Its habitual route in the era before the opening of the Suez Canal was from Gravesend along the Channel to France, then due south past Spain and following the African west coast to Cape Town; from there the ship crossed the Indian Ocean to Madras and Calcutta. Often the ship stopped at Portsmouth as well on the way out. The ship carried a number of high-profile passengers during the late 1830s, especially senior military figures such as Major-General Sir John Doveton and the Commander-in-Chief of Madras, Sir Peregrine Maitland. In July 1838, the *True Briton* took the Scottish minister and philosopher Henry Caldrewood to take up a missionary role in South Africa. During their first night at sea on this particular voyage, there was a dramatic incident that must have alarmed the relatively inexperienced Midshipman Martin and frightened the passengers. It was very foggy in the English Channel, which was the busiest stretch of water in the world, and in the murky darkness a Norwegian vessel ran into the *True Briton* without warning and caused considerable damage. The ship had to return to port and required a week's repair work before it could set sail once more. On the same voyage a Mrs Hamond, whose husband was a captain in the Madras Artillery, suddenly gave birth to a daughter on 20 October, so the young Midshipman Martin was exposed to his fair share of surprises.

Martin completed his training and was appointed as a junior officer by the Wigrams. He may have served briefly on their ship *Southampton* but, by 1841, John Martin was third officer aboard the *Maidstone*, where he served under the celebrated Captain John Thomas Nash. The *Maidstone* sailed to India, and contemporary adverts for Wigram ships show that the company was still aiming at the high end of the market – the vessels are described as 'superior first-class'. Under Nash's leadership, John Martin thrived. He rose through the ranks on the *Maidstone* from third mate, to second mate, to first mate.

When Martin was appointed to his first command, it is not surprising that he was earmarked for the captain's role on a ship on the India route. The *Hampshire* was newly launched, and Money Wigram & Sons even posted adverts advising that John Martin was her captain. But then, abruptly, they changed their minds: a new captain on a new ship seemed unwise. Captain

---

SHIPPING.

1843.

The following superior FIRST-CLASS SHIPS, belonging to Messrs. WIGRAM, of Blackwall Yard, built and fitted purposely for the INDIA TRADE, will leave GRAVESEND at the appointed dates.

Each Ship carries an experienced Surgeon.

For MADRAS and CALCUTTA :–

	Tons.	Commanders.	
ESSEX	850	W. H. BREWER	June 15

For the CAPE and CALCUTTA :–

	Tons.	Commanders.	
MAIDSTONE	1000	J. T. NASH	July 10

For CALCUTTA direct :–

	Tons.	Commanders.	
SOUTHAMPTON	1050	W. A. BOWEN	July 25
QUEEN	1350	DONALD McLEOD	Sept. 5

For the CAPE and MADRAS :–

	Tons.	Commanders.	
TRUE BRITON	800	C. C. CONSITT	

For Freight or Passage, apply to the respective Commanders, at the Jerusalem Coffee-House ; and to WIMBLE and ALLPORT, with Messrs. WIGRAM, 89, Gracechurch Street, corner of Leadenhall Street.

Newspaper advert for Money Wigram ships to India in 1843.

Madras in India was an important destination for British trade and military personnel.

Martin's views on this *volte-face* are not recorded. Instead, in early 1852, John Martin was given command of the *Essex*. This was a smaller vessel than he had been used to – about the same size as the *True Briton* – and it was thirteen years old, but importantly this ship was the first under his command to sail the route to Australia. Captain Martin was trusted to sail this much longer and unfamiliar route without any prior experience, which was perhaps a tribute to his ability. However, having passed him over for the plum role of master of a brand-new ship, Money Wigram & Sons had to quickly find him an alternative. Yet, evidently, Captain Martin did very well in this position and, after four years on the *Essex*, he was transferred to the *Suffolk*, the biggest 'pure' sailing ship he would command, at 976 tons, and a newly built vessel designed for the Australia run. The *Suffolk* would also be Captain Martin's lengthiest command as he was in charge of this vessel for eight years. During this time he built a name for himself as a captain who delivered a reliable, comfortable, safe, and speedy cruise.

The *Suffolk* acquired a justified reputation as a consistently fast ship, and the accommodation for passengers on board was described by the press as 'remarkably good'. Consequently the *Suffolk* began to be sought after by persons of importance. For example, governors sent to Australia by the British, such as Sir Dominick Daly and Sir Charles Darling, chose the *Suffolk* when they sailed out to take up their appointments. It must have been particularly satisfying for Captain Martin to demonstrate his ship's fine sailing qualities to these influential people.

Even in bad weather the *Suffolk* could make a good time. On Captain Martin's first voyage to Australia in 1857, the ship was caught in severe weather on 10 June and, according to a published extract of Captain

Captain Martin served on the Wigram ship *Essex*. (Brodie Collection, La Trobe Picture Collection, State Library of Victoria)

Martin's log, the vessel lost its entire foremast and bowsprit. The hasty repairs at sea involved creating improvised replacements for both masts made from timber on board; usually spare yards were used to construct stumpy substitutes. Despite this, the jury-rigged *Suffolk* still managed to complete its journey in eighty-two days. The skill and energy shown by Captain Martin in reaching Australia in such a good time, despite the damage, earned him considerable respect. Upon his return to England, the mercantile portion of the City of London presented him with a handsome testimonial as a mark of their esteem, which included a gift of £500. This was a generous sum. Only fifteen years before, Martin had been earning a mere £3 per month when he took up his post as third mate on the *Maidstone*.

There is an amusing story connected with this first voyage of the *Suffolk*, one that says something about Captain Martin's personality. While the *Suffolk* was hove to in a damaged condition after the storm, an American vessel came up within hailing distance. Seeing the crew frantically repairing the *Suffolk*, the US captain offered assistance and, when this was politely declined, he offered to report the ship when he reached Melbourne. This was usual practice in the nineteenth century. A vessel docking at port would notify the authorities of ships seen en route, particularly those in distress, in case the ship should be delayed or lost. Captain Martin was confident in his ship's speed, despite the damage, and joked that, after completing his repairs to *Suffolk*, it would be Martin who would report the American vessel. When the American captain reached Port Phillip, Melbourne, he called on the local agents for the *Suffolk* to let them know that their ship might be delayed because of storm damage. He was astounded when the agents told him that Captain Martin was in the room next door and had arrived five days ago.

Melbourne became a familiar destination for Captain Martin. (Engraving by Samuel Calvert, courtesy of State Library of Victoria)

Captain Martin made ten voyages to Australia and back during the eight years he was in command of the *Suffolk*, and the ship acquired a certain celebrity on account of her habitually rapid journey times. An article in Melbourne newspaper *The Leader* in 1863 described the *Suffolk*'s place among Money Wigram's array of ships as 'the yacht of the fleet, from her great length and remarkable sailing qualities'. The reporter goes on to describe that 'another cause of her celebrity has been the average brevity of her passages, that have ranged from sixty-eight to seventy-eight days, the greater number having been completed in from sixty-nine to seventy-two. Of the last four outward passages two have occupied only sixty-nine days'. More importantly, these speedy runs occurred without any serious incident, other than during Captain Martin's first voyage. Martin had become, as one author noted, 'a captain whose good fortune had become almost proverbial'.

Appointment to the *London*

In one sense it was an easy decision for Wigram & Sons when they came to consider the position of captain for the SS *London*. They were looking for a reliable company man with a reputation that would attract passengers, and considerable experience of the Australia run. Captain Martin ticked all the boxes.

There is no reason to doubt his seafaring skills as the master of a sailing vessel; however, until he became master of the *London*, John Martin had never set foot on a steamship, let alone commanded one. Despite commercial steamships existing since the late 1830s, all of his professional experience was under sail. Nevertheless, the Wigrams were loyal to their captains, and preferred employing 'company men' – officers that it knew and had trained. All of this meant that, when it came to appointing a captain for the new SS *London*, no thought seems to have been given to recruiting a ship's master who already had steamship experience.

We none of us know how we will behave in a catastrophe until we find ourselves in the middle of one. However, some experience of similar situations helps. Before the fateful day in 1866 when the *London* sank beneath his feet, John Martin had been aboard a ship in danger only twice in his thirty-year career: a collision with a vessel as a midshipman in 1838, and one heavy storm on the *Suffolk* in 1857, causing the ship to lose its foremast and bowsprit, which he dealt with competently. It might be said that good captains avoided crises, which to a certain extent could be true, but even the best seafarers cannot avoid the vagaries of the weather.

So, although Captain Martin's appointment may have been the obvious choice for Money Wigram & Sons, he was not perhaps the best choice. He had no experience of commanding steamships on his appointment or of handling vessels over 1,000 tons, and very limited experience of handling a ship in danger. Consequently, when faced with the double problem of a less familiar ship in serious difficulties, as he was on the *London* in January 1866, it is not surprising that he may have made mistakes. Unfortunately, during those hours he would have no fellow officers to turn to who could help him because they had even less experience than himself.

Life as a Captain

The captain's role on a nineteenth-century passenger ship was not simply confined to managing the crew and the ship. The ideal captain was of course a first-class seaman and leader of men, but he was also a charming and intelligent gentleman who could interact well with the passengers. Victorian newspaper adverts for sailings in the 1860s always gave emphasis to the captain as well as the ship. One was never mentioned without the other.

This is especially apparent in the (then) British colonies that depended upon commercial shipping for their communication with the rest of the world. Accordingly, their newspapers were quick to praise ships' captains that provided a good service. As a typical example, Melbourne newspaper *The Age* had this to say about Captain Martin in 1855: 'A gentleman much and deservedly esteemed by those who have accompanied him on former passages to and from Australia'. Naturally, the various accounts of John Martin published after his death also extolled his virtues. His obituary in the *Illustrated London News*, for instance, described him as 'an officer of high reputation'.

Gerard Moultrie wrote a book entitled *Wreck of the 'London'* within a few weeks of the ship's loss. He claims to have spoken to many who knew the *London*'s master and Moultrie says of him:

> Many are still living who crossed the seas with him [on the *Suffolk*] ... who will recall with pleasure his practised skill, his genial, open disposition, his gentlemanly bearing and his studious care for the comfort of his

passengers in all the little details which have so much to do with the making or marring of the pleasure of a long voyage.

The captain on a medium-to-large passenger ship had spacious accommodation for himself, which would have typically comprised a suite of rooms: a day cabin with a table where he could entertain a meeting or a small selection of guests, an office area with a desk for writing, and his sleeping quarters. It was not unusual for a captain to take his wife away to sea with him, so there was often room for more than one sleeper.

A ship's captain was expected to dine with First Class passengers on a regular basis. Eating at the captain's table was a privilege that the most important passengers on board expected, and which others aspired to. Usually the captain would dine at table in the First Class saloon, but he might receive especially distinguished guests for meals privately in his own cabin. Other officers were also expected to dine with passengers and, during a long voyage, might rotate around the passengers' tables to meet and converse with as many of them as possible. Moultrie reports that Captain Martin was known to keep 'one of the best and most hospitable of tables for those on board his ship'. He also suggests that the captain never drank spirits: 'only once in his life did he taste a small quantity of spirits, but the alcohol had such an effect upon him that he never repeated the experiment'. However, as noted in an earlier chapter, the Victorians had low expectations of the moral character of seamen, and so when holding up Captain Martin as a moral example – as the book does – it would have been important to establish his temperance credentials.

Other duties for the captain were not so pleasant. If anyone died on board, he had to conduct the funeral, and dispose of the body at sea unless

A captain's cabin.

the ship was close to a port: in the days before refrigeration, there was simply nowhere to store a body safely. Captains also had to discipline the crew, take responsibility for the ship's paperwork, deal with stowaways, and manage any dissent or bad behaviour among the passengers.

But what was Captain Martin like as a person – as a man, rather than a ship's captain? We can learn from various sources that he was unmarried, and that physically he was of medium height, with blue eyes, a fresh-coloured face, light hair, and a cheery voice but slow manner of speaking. He was a busy man at sea, but when ashore he particularly liked to sit around and read the newspaper. Moultrie reports that, like many sailors, Captain Martin had an ambling gait; was very superstitious and fond of cats; and loved his ship. How much of this is really true, or simply Moultrie's exploitation of the popular stereotype of seafaring men prevalent at the time, is impossible to say. He reports that the captain had a reputation as a thoughtful person, and there is some evidence to support this from his actions in the dying minutes of the SS *London*. The author also notes a peculiarly personal character trait: Captain Martin delighted in riddles.

There is one final point to note about Captain Martin. The SS *London*'s registration documents clearly show that he personally invested in the ship. Vessels were traditionally divided into sixty-four parts as far as ownership was concerned and the *London* ownership was as follows:

Charles Hampden Wigram, Clifford Wigram, and Robert Wigram – fifty-six shares
John Bohun Martin – four shares
Franklin Allport – two shares
Charles Morgan – two shares

A ship's captain conducts a burial at sea.

It is not surprising that members of the Wigram family owned the vast majority of shares in the ship. Allport and Morgan were the ship brokers who sold tickets to passengers and helped to secure cargoes for the ship, so in business terms it made sense that they had an interest in the profitability of each voyage. It acted as an incentive for them. However, the captain's role is so intimately associated with the safety of passengers and crew that a financial interest could be seen as a potential conflict of interest. Captain Martin's four shares meant that he would receive one-sixteenth of the profits of the voyage. This was not unusual at the time and, indeed, Captain Martin had invested in the ownership of his previous ship the *Suffolk* as well, owning eight shares of the ship. All the same, when crucial decisions were made about safety, the captain must always have had one eye on his interest in the ship's commercial success. Did profit cloud his professional judgement as a seaman?

6
The Passengers

The SS *London* could accommodate 400 passengers, but on its final voyage the ship carried only 164 named fare-paying passengers (see Appendix 1). No contemporary source comments on why so few people were apparently on board this prestigious ship. For the poorer classes of passenger – those in Third Class and Steerage – shipping companies often failed to keep wholly accurate records because these lowly people were not important as long as they had paid their fare. So the list of First and Second Class passengers is easier to construct, and probably accurate, especially since journalists in Australia would demand a list of them to publish in local newspapers on arrival. Strangely, we learn that at least one passenger, Fanny Batchelor, only managed to secure a berth at the last moment due to a cancellation, suggesting the ship was 'full', and we also know that some space originally intended for accommodation was given over to cargo. In addition, a dozen or so passengers did not arrive in time for departure. But, surely, poor record-keeping, latecomers, and storage of excess cargo cannot account for 236 empty berths? This is a mystery; but perhaps business was not booming.

Those who booked passage on the *London* were a mixture of British and Australian residents. The owners were keen to trumpet the luxury and speed of the SS *London* in the promotional literature issued for the third voyage:

> This magnificent Steam Ship, built and fitted expressly for the passenger trade to Australia, has just performed the passage from Plymouth to Melbourne in 60 days ... Her accommodations for all classes of passengers are unsurpassed.

The Wigrams also noted that 'a large stock of medical comforts will be put on board, and dispensed according to the directions of the surgeon'.

Passengers had to book their place with the owners' agents Allport and Morgan of Leadenhall Street, London, to whom they could write or apply in person. The alternative means of securing a ticket was to speak to Captain Martin while the ship was in East India Dock. Half the fare had to be paid

OUTWARD PASSAGE SIXTY DAYS.
1865.

STEAM FROM
LONDON TO MELBOURNE

MESSRS. **MONEY WIGRAM & SONS'**,
Of Blackwall Yard, London,
Line of Steam and Packet Ships to Australia.

To leave the **EAST INDIA DOCKS** on Thursday, 28th December,
CALLING AT PLYMOUTH,
FOR
MELBOURNE,
Landing Passengers and their Baggage on the Wharf free of charge; also, if required, forwarding them by Steam to Geelong, Sydney, Adelaide, Launceston, Hobart Town, and New Zealand,
For which a separate arrangement must be made.

THE SPLENDID NEW AUXILIARY SCREW STEAM-SHIP
"LONDON"
1,752 Tons Register.   200 Horse Power Nominal.   800 Indicated.
J. BOHUN MARTIN, COMMANDER.
Built by, and belonging to, Messrs. Money Wigram & Sons, of Blackwall.
LYING IN THE EAST INDIA DOCKS.

This magnificent Steam Ship, built and fitted expressly for the Passenger Trade to AUSTRALIA has just performed the Passage from PLYMOUTH TO MELBOURNE in 60 Days. She has been specially constructed to form one of the above celebrated Line of Packet Ships, which comprises the **Lincolnshire, Essex, Yorkshire, Suffolk, Norfolk, Sussex, Kent, True Briton,** and other fast, favorite, and well-known Ships. Her accommodations for all classes of Passengers are unsurpassed, and she will carry an experienced Surgeon.

Original sailing brochure for SS *London*'s final voyage.

in advance and the balance was due three days before departure. Prices were the same whether a passenger embarked at London or Plymouth, but children under twelve years of age were half price and infants under one year were carried free.

Those who wished to travel could choose between four classes of accommodation: First Class (known as 'saloon class'), Second Class, Third Class, and Steerage. All were provided with cooked food during the voyage. The fares varied to reflect the luxury, size, location, and privacy of accommodation; the quality and amount of food available; the access to privileged areas of the ship; and the quantity of luggage that could be taken on board (40 cubic feet for First Class; 15 for Third Class and Steerage).

The ship plans for the SS *London* have not survived, so the exact location and distribution of the various berths for passengers are not known with complete certainty. However, from various sources such as the ship's log, press coverage, advertisements, and the designs of similar ships, it is known that all First Class passengers were accommodated on the main deck. Some had berths in a cabin house near the mainmast, but the majority were located beneath the poop and in close proximity to the First Class saloon and dining area. There were fifty-nine First Class passengers on board for the *London*'s final voyage.

The fare for a First Class passenger could be up to five times greater than that charged to someone travelling in Steerage, and so attracted relatively wealthy people. The price varied primarily according to the cabin's size and location. All of the cabins were small by modern standards, but an individual who took the smallest and least favoured berth in the main-deck cabin paid sixty guineas per person; the largest and best appointed cabins – or state rooms – were under the poop and were the most expensive, costing seventy-five guineas.

The owners were keen to point out that First Class passengers would be provided with everything they needed for the voyage including 'berths, beds, bedding linen, plate, table linen etc.' The food for the voyage was boldly described as 'excellent' but, although a First Class ticket included the cost of the stewards attending passengers, it did not include 'wines, spirits, or malt liquors, which may be purchased on board at fixed moderate rates'. First Class passengers were allowed to visit every public area of the ship, and had exclusive use of the poop deck and the elegant First Class saloon with its lofty glass skylights.

Second Class passengers paid twenty-five to thirty guineas for the voyage. They were accommodated on the lower deck, roughly amidships, and on the main deck under the forecastle, where there was also a separate saloon. The promotional brochure for the SS *London* reminded travellers that

> Second class passengers are required to furnish themselves with mattress, bedding, linen etc. They are supplied with knives, forks, crockery, etc. by the ship, and provided with steward's attendance, but are expected to promote their own and each other's comfort by assisting as far as possible.

The main attraction to travelling Second Class was the privacy afforded by separate cabins, and the better calibre of meals than those in Third Class. Having said this, passengers were instructed that, if they travelled alone, they could not object to sharing a two-berth cabin with a stranger of the same sex. All the passengers apart from First Class effectively had food 'rations', and the owners published quotas showing what every person on board could expect to receive while at sea. For Second Class, the weekly indicative scale of victualling for every adult passenger is shown below:

1 lb preserved meat	1 pint preserved milk	6 oz lime juice
1 lb soup and bouilli	1 lb sugar	½ oz mustard
1 pint assorted soups	2 oz tea	½ ox pepper
½ lb preserved or salt fish	½ lb coffee	1 oz salt
1½ lb salt beef or pork	½ lb butter	7 lbs potatoes,
1 lb rice	½ lb cheese	or 1lb preserved ditto
4 lb bread	1 lb raisins or currants	21 quarts of water
3 lb flour	¾ lb suet	7 pints porter
½ pint peas	½ pint pickles or vinegar	1 bottle of wine, to adults

These rations were prepared into meals that were cooked and served on board, but the victualling scales gave passengers an idea what they were paying for and also imposed limits on what the ship had to provide. On the last voyage of the *London*, there were fifty-two Second Class passengers on board.

The differentiation between Third Class and Steerage in the nineteenth century was inconsistent, and depended on the attitudes of the ship's owners and the space available on the vessel. Some ships did not have a Third Class; some did not admit Steerage passengers.

The fifty-three Third Class passengers on the *London* paid between eighteen and twenty guineas to travel and were reminded that they 'must provide their own bedding, mess utensils etc., such as mattress, blankets, knives, forks, spoons, plates, dishes etc.' Their accommodation would probably have been in less private berths on the lower deck, and their access to the main deck may well have been restricted so that they did not frequently mix with First and Second Class passengers. There were victualling rates for Third Class passengers that were significantly less generous than those allocated to Second Class.

SCALE OF VICTUALLING FOR THIRD CABIN PASSENGERS.

FOR EACH ADULT THIRD CABIN PASSENGER.

Victualling rates for Third Class passengers on the *London*.

Steerage passengers would certainly have slept in hammocks, and these would have been squeezed into a single dormitory-style area on the lower deck with no privacy. The policy of Money Wigram & Sons towards Steerage is clear in its advertising – namely that, because there was no room to segregate the sexes, the SS *London* would carry only men in its Steerage compartment.

Although advertising for the SS *London* encourages Steerage passengers to travel, none of the contemporary accounts of the ship's final voyage identify a single Steerage passenger by name. This might be because the owners only took these passengers at the last minute if there was room, or that the Steerage fare on the SS *London* (fifteen guineas) was more expensive than alternative ships so that people were unlikely to choose the vessel. To put this fare into perspective, a labourer in the mid-1860s might earn about £2 per month, so a one-way trip to Australia would cost about eight month's wages. It may be that no Steerage passengers embarked on the final voyage, but it is also possible that no-one kept a list of them.

The cheapest way for an impoverished person to go abroad was not to pay a fare, but to become a stowaway. There were stowaways on board the *London*, as survivor James Wilson recalled: 'I was told of some, and I knew of three on board whose names were not on the published list; say there were six'. Stowaways were relatively common, but it was a risky pursuit. Some captains angrily sent them ashore as soon as possible after they were discovered, leaving them stranded perhaps hundreds or thousands of miles from home; other captains would arrest them for later prosecution. A stowaway was almost inevitably caught and relied upon a benevolent captain allowing them to 'work their passage' – that is, performing suitable duties during the voyage without payment in exchange for travel to the final destination, food and accommodation while on board. In 1883, for example, passenger William Lilley on a voyage to Australia describes the fate of a stowaway on the SS *Orient*:

> The talk this morning on deck was about the finding of a stowaway. A young fellow looking very much like a London costermonger was found hidden behind the boiler. He was brought out and taken to the captain who, after questioning him, decided that he should be allowed to work his passage out to Sydney … As I went past the engine-room about eight o'clock, I found him working away with a will, cleaning the brass-work, well content with his lot. He told me that he was unmarried and he hoped, after he had worked his passage out, to do better in the new country than in the old. Sometimes as many as nine or ten stowaways have been found on board this ship. Generally these poor fellows have friends among the seamen, and sometimes their presence on board is connived at by the mates of the ship, as in that way they can get an extra hand or two at little cost.

Reasons for Travel

The *London*'s passengers travelled for all sorts of reasons. Many were either new emigrants to Australia, or had returned briefly to the UK for some business or family purpose. A group of ten people from Cumberland, for example, were travelling together in order to settle permanently in Australia. William, Thomas and David Graham were brothers and they were taking their families and two friends to Australia. Thomas and David had been farming there for some time and had returned to England to buy equipment and seek business advice. They also came back to visit family, and to encourage relations to join them. Their younger brother William wanted to emigrate, but could not afford it – he would have had to pay for his wife and three children, too, one of whom was a four-month-old baby. Thomas generously paid all their fares, and the five of them travelled in Third Class together with a family friend and a cousin.

Thomas had had another reason for returning to England: to marry his sweetheart Mary Bruce, and this ceremony was completed just three weeks before they stepped on to the *London* for their voyage to Melbourne. The party of ten left Cumberland on 27 December by train, and a large number of friends gathered to see them off; they were given three cheers as the steam engine left the station.

Emigration was a well-known means to escape the poverty trap for underpaid and exploited workers such as agricultural labourers. However, it was not just the poor who emigrated in order to work: John Debenham was the son of William Debenham, the founder of Debenhams department stores. He was travelling on board the *London* with his wife, Emily, to work in Australia as an engineer. Needless to say, they travelled First Class.

Emigrants reaching Australia after their long voyage.

A number of the passengers were British-born goldminers who had done well for themselves in Australia, but had returned to their home country to visit family and friends. John Hickman, for example, had already been so successful after a short spell in Ballarat that he went back to the UK to collect his wife, Jane, and four children to return with him. Fellow travellers John Munro, John Wilson, and David Main were also miners. John Munro was a thirty-six-year-old Scot who knew John Hickman well as he lived nearby in Ballarat. He had been a sailmaker on various ships for five-and-a-half years before emigrating, and so was very familiar with the dangers of travel by sea. During his seagoing days he had been shipwrecked off the coast of Central America, and was trapped there penniless for months while he tried to get back home.

In a world where shipwrecks were commonplace, it should not be surprising that other passengers are known to have been involved in accidents at sea. Henry Dennis was a colonial explorer, and in March 1861 he was on board the clipper *Marco Polo* in the Southern Ocean when it struck an iceberg in the middle of the night. Chaos ensued as it was immediately assumed that the shattered bows of the ship would cause it to sink but, by some miracle, the vessel and all aboard survived. Dennis was a remarkable man who seemed to court danger; in the midst of the American Civil War he had provoked his neighbours in the southern states by running his cotton plantation using paid black employees instead of slaves.

Another passenger, Alan Sandilands, was recognised by seaman John King as a fellow survivor of the notorious wreck of the *Duncan Dunbar* off the coast of Brazil just a few months previously in October 1865. Newspaper reports suggest that there were other survivors of the *Duncan Dunbar* on board as well, but they are not identified.

Passengers David Main (left), John Munro (seated), and James Wilson (right) went to Australia to work as miners.

Some passengers were travelling for health purposes. George Palmer, for example, was a barrister and editor of the professional periodical *The Law Review*, but he had suffered for some time with a chest complaint. It was common for Victorian doctors to advise their patients to take a long sea voyage to ease a chronic lung problem as sea air was believed to be healthy, and the voyage encouraged patients to rest. A warmer climate at the destination also proved beneficial to many sufferers. Palmer had decided to work in Australia for at least a year to see if this improved matters. Mr and Mrs Clark had emigrated from the UK over thirty years previously, but had come to England to seek specialist medical treatment for their twenty-one-year-old son, George. He had suffered since childhood with a diseased arm but, to their joy, he was successfully operated upon in London and full function was restored. They were thus returning to Australia to be reunited with their family.

Gustavus Vaughan Brooke had very different reasons for travelling. He was a recognised Shakespearian actor, who had been successful in the past but, fuelled by heavy drinking and a dissipated life, his career was on the wane. His agent, in an attempt to revitalise his fortunes managed to secure him roles in Australia where he was still held in high regard after a series of much-acclaimed performances earlier in his life. Rumour had it that he also had heavy debts, and leaving the country was one way to avoid imprisonment. Some credibility can be attached to these suspicions, by the fact that he and his sister travelled together anonymously as 'Mr and Mrs Vaughan', an alias that might avoid drawing attention to the well-known actor with his distinctive name. The passenger list furnished by Money Wigram & Sons clearly shows that the 'Mr and Mrs Vaughan' entry was subsequently changed: 'Mrs' was later crossed out and changed to 'Miss', and 'Brooke' was added afterwards in brackets. In a posthumous account of the actor's life, his biographer William Lawrence had this to say about the manner of his departure on the *London*:

> As Brooke was not the man to travel incognito from mere motives of delicacy, the only reason that can be assigned for the course pursued was the natural desire to escape from the pressing attention of his creditors. Whether this be true or not, a legend exists to the effect that Brooke had some difficulty in getting on board without arrest, and even then thought it advisable to lie *perdu* until the anchor was lifted. The story goes that two sheriffs' officers clambered up the vessel at the eleventh hour and informed Captain Martin they had warrants for the arrest of the tragedian, of whose whereabouts they were perfectly assured. Nothing daunted by a fruitless scrutiny of the passenger list, these vigilant worthies demanded the commander's assistance in the execution of their duty ... Then began a vigorous search, but all to no purpose ... And what of Brooke during this anxious period? No sooner was the coast clear than he is said to have emerged from the forecastle disguised as a sailor, only to utter profuse expressions of gratitude in a choked voice to the gallant, warm-hearted commander.

Gustavus Vaughan Brooke as Iago in Shakespeare's *Othello*.

Henry Samuel Chapman was a judge at the Supreme Court of New Zealand, based at Dunedin. He did not travel on the SS *London*, but his wife, Catherine or 'Kitty', and three of his children were on board. They had travelled to England to leave one of their sons behind; Frederick was to complete his higher education in the UK. At the same time, Mrs Chapman collected her older son, Harry, who had finished his tuition. The judge's wife also had another mission. She was to pick up a valuable inheritance that was due to her husband when his Aunt Fanny died. This elderly relative was then in her nineties, but not expected to live much longer, and she was keen that a fortune in jewellery be handed over to her nephew's family in person.

There were three clergymen on board, and they were to prove important characters in the telling of the *London*'s last hours. Daniel Draper was a Methodist minister from Wickham, in Hampshire, who had originally sailed to Australia in 1835 as a missionary. He had travelled widely, to Sydney, Adelaide, Parramatta and Melbourne to name but a few places. After thirty years in Australia, he and his wife returned to England so that he might attend the annual Methodist conference and to visit family and friends. Six months later he booked his return passage on the SS *London*, eager to resume his missionary work among the working men of Australia. The Drapers were with some fifty or so other passengers who embarked at Plymouth. Moultrie reproduces a letter that Draper wrote to a friend, shortly before departure:

> The steamer (the *London*) is a fine new vessel, having gone out but twice. Last time she did the voyage in sixty days. We join her (god willing) at

Revd Daniel Draper.

Plymouth on 2nd January, and she will leave that port at 6pm on that day. We trust in God our Heavenly Father for protection on our way, and delight in the thought that we shall be remembered by kind friends when they bow at the throne of grace.

The two other ministers were Revd Dr John Woolley, Principal in Classics and Logic at the University of Sydney, and Revd James Kerr from Armadale in West Lothian.

So, the *London*'s passengers had many reasons to get to Australia – to escape the poverty trap, start a new life, seek a change of employment, be reunited with family, take home valuable assets, improve their health, preach the word of God, and even to escape their debts. This collection of people was therefore a cross section of Victorian society and, once the voyage began, they were all eager for it to be over as soon as possible. After leaving Plymouth, they would not see land again until nearly at Melbourne. Two months was a long time to spend at sea and, with no organised entertainment on board, there would be little to do from one day to the next except to talk, walk, read and write, eat, pray, and sleep.

Life on Board

Passenger Samuel Smiles travelled by a Money Wigram ship in 1869 and describes a typical day on his ship, the *Yorkshire*:

> At about six every morning we are roused by the sailors holystoning the decks, under the superintendence of the officer of the watch. A couple

of middies pump up water from the sea, by means of a pump placed just behind the wheel. It fills the tub until it overflows, running along the scuppers of the poop, and out on to the main-deck through a pipe. Here the seamen fill their buckets, and proceed with the scouring of the main-deck. Such a scrubbing and mopping!

By the time the passengers dressed and went on deck the cleaning process was over, and the decks were dry. After half an hour's pacing the poop the bell would ring for breakfast, the appetite for which would depend very much upon the state of the weather and the lurching of the ship. Between breakfast and lunch, more promenading on the poop; the passengers sometimes, if the weather was fine, forming themselves in groups on deck, cultivating each other's acquaintance.

We lunched at twelve. From thence, until dinner at five, we mooned about on deck as before, or visited sick passengers, or read in our respective cabins, or passed the time in conversation; and thus the day wore on. After dinner the passengers drew together in parties and became social. In the pleasantly-lit saloon some of the elder subsided into whist, while the juniors sought the middies in their cabin on the main-deck, next door to the sheep-pen; there they entertained themselves and each other with songs, accompanied by the concertina and clouds of tobacco-smoke.

These fixed parts of the day were accompanied by other activities. Watching wildlife was popular – whales, dolphins, birds, and flying fish – and

It was common for passengers to kill albatrosses for trophies when sailing to Australia.

catching or shooting seabirds such as albatrosses was a well-known activity; they were killed to make trophies or for sport. There were wagers on how many miles the ship would sail each day; frequently there was the opportunity to admire a wonderful sunset at sea; on Sunday there might be a church service; and passengers commonly organised for themselves little concerts or talent contests where individuals acted, read aloud, sang or played instruments. There were some gentle deck games such as quoits, and energetic passengers might climb the rigging, sometimes pursued by crewmen who would tie them down and only release them on payment of a forfeit. Writing letters home was popular, with ships looking out eagerly for homeward-bound vessels that might take these letters back to the UK. The weather could be very trying for passengers – from the blazing humid heat of the tropics to listless calms, or lengthy storms that threw everyone around in their confines below.

Most passengers developed a routine centred around meal times, and gradually adapted to the slow pace of life on board ship; but within a few weeks they were all eager to reach their destination and get back to land. There was traditionally a splendid final meal on board on the last night at sea, in which the captain thanked the passengers and they, in turn, thanked him and the crew.

Yet despite all that passengers and crew did to try and keep day-to-day life interesting, everyone knew that a long voyage soon became rather mundane, and this is why faster ships like the SS *London* were so popular.

7
The Final Voyage

The SS *London* made just two round trips to Australia before it was overtaken by disaster in early 1866. So the ship was still practically new. Yet it had begun to establish a good reputation for luxury and speed, and no-one could have anticipated that the *London*'s third voyage to Melbourne would be its last.

Preparation for this final journey was the same as for the previous two. Given the owners' close association with the East India Company, the ships of Money Wigram & Sons departed from that company's former home: the East India Docks were conveniently located a short distance down river from the Blackwall yards, where Wigram ships were built.

The East India Docks had been built in the early nineteenth century and were connected to the River Thames by a large basin that allowed ships to enter or leave via lock gates. This basin connected two inner docks – an import dock where goods brought into the country by ship were taken off, and an export dock where cargo was loaded and passengers could board. Hence it was at the export dock that the SS *London* prepared for departure in December 1865.

The *London*'s cargo was loaded over a period of days before any passengers took up residence. The hatchways were opened up and waterside cranes or 'derricks' hoisted swinging loads from the dockside and lowered them carefully into the *London*'s hold under guidance from the ship's crew. It was a noisy time: winches, pulleys, thumps and heaves from down below, and the constant shouting of instructions. Everything entering the hold had to be placed prudently to ensure it didn't become dislodged during the voyage and that the ship kept its trim at sea.

The final cargo consisted of approximately 950 tons of 'light goods', items such as textiles, china, and drugs; about 345 tons of 'dead weight' such as iron, and stone blocks; and a further 14 tons or so of agricultural implements, hardware and so forth. It was a typical mixed cargo bound for a rapidly expanding Australian colony, and slightly less than the ship had carried on her second voyage. Its value was estimated at £124,785 17*s* 4*d* and it took six days to load it all, under the careful supervision of the

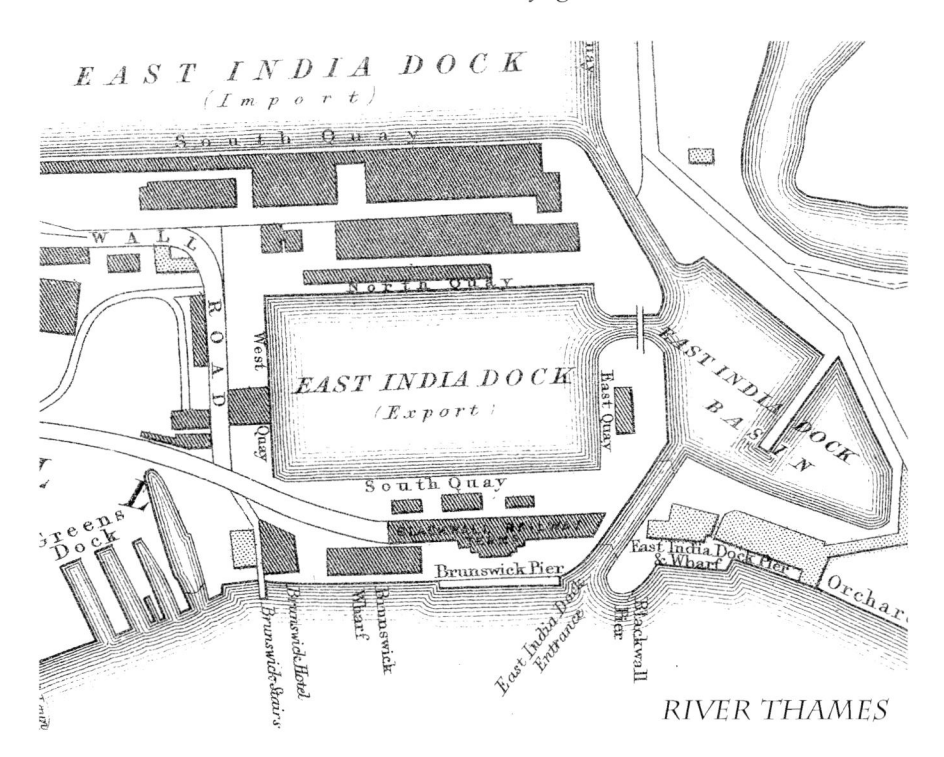

Map from 1866 showing East India Docks.

ship's second officer, Arthur Ticehurst, who stayed in the hold the whole time. The importance of the cargo to the financial success of the voyage is borne out by the fact that one of Money Wigram's sons, Clifford, was present the whole time. Every inch of space not used was money wasted.

In addition to all this weight, the *London* required around 500 tons of coal as fuel and 200 tons of iron kentledge ('ballast'). Coal was loaded from designated coaling vessels on the Thames; there were no scheduled refuelling stops *en route*, so the coal loaded now had to last until Melbourne. Many sacks of coal had to be stored on the main deck. This was perhaps partly because coal stored too close to the hot boilers in the hold had caught fire on the first voyage, but the *London* was also crammed with cargo, leaving insufficient room below decks.

Finally, some of the ship's provisions for the voyage were loaded – food, water, alcoholic beverages, fresh linen and so forth. These amounted to some 120 tons.

Once the ship's cargo was aboard and the vessel refuelled, the crew began the task of readying the *London* for her passengers. The decks were hosed down to wash away the mess generated from cargo and coal; the planking was scrubbed, portholes cleaned, brass polished, cabins swept out, lanterns charged with oil, and fresh linen provided. This was also an opportunity to attend to any damaged paintwork or minor repairs.

Ships in dock preparing to sail formed a temporary community of souls. Crewmen on neighbouring ships chatted together, socialised, drank, smoked, and even competed with one another. At the beginning of the twentieth century, Seaman William Caius Crutchley was able to look back and recall an example of that community spirit:

> What is known as 'taking the time ball' was one of the events of the day. A midshipman belonging to each vessel would be perched in some prominent part of the poop of each ship, and in close proximity would be the boatswain and his mates, ready to pipe to dinner and grog at the instant the signal was given that the ball had dropped. The chorus of pipes was a thing to hear and remember, as it was taken up by the assembled ships; there was always a laudable ambition to be the first ship to commence.

But it was not all plain sailing. Six seamen who had agreed to join the *London* decided against it at the last minute. Antonio Margarella, Walter Fortune, Martin Rooks, Anthony Dougharty, Edward Allen and William Johnson must have thought that providence was on their side when they later discovered the fate of the ship. Yet at the time, this must have been a serious nuisance to Captain Martin, who had no time to find replacements before the ship sailed.

Passengers Arrive

Many of the passengers embarked at the East India Docks on Thursday 28 December 1865. Friends and relatives came to see them off and would have been allowed on board to make their farewells. When the ship was ready to depart, a seaman paced the vessel ringing a bell and shouting 'strangers ashore' to encourage any stragglers to leave. The gangplank was raised, the *London* was towed from her berth by steam tugs into the basin and then, at high tide, the lock system enabled the ship to enter the Thames.

Little remains of the East India Docks today; the export and import docks were filled in and have been built over. However, miraculously, the basin that the SS *London* passed through has survived. The lock gates, and the channel they sit in, are not the same as they were in 1866, but there is some satisfaction to be had in visiting this site opposite the Millennium Dome on the Thames, and contemplating the *London*'s tragic final voyage at the place where it actually began.

Meanwhile, the new passengers on the *London* were busy locating their cabins and stowing away their luggage. They also had to find the steward, decide the time at which they wished to eat their evening meal and select their seat in the dining area; choices they had to stick with for the entire voyage. Once this was complete, passengers could relax and explore the ship.

An important individual had also boarded the ship at East India Docks. George Thompson was the Trinity House pilot, engaged to navigate the

Loading the passengers' luggage.

The East India Docks basin is still in place and now acts as a wildlife haven.

London down the Thames and then all the way to Plymouth, where a local pilot would assume responsibility for taking the vessel to a safe mooring.

Under Thompson's direction, the *London* made its way down the river to Gravesend in Kent, where more passengers joined, together with the remainder of the ship's provisions. Samuel Smiles, who travelled on a Money Wigram ship in 1869, described the scene at Gravesend:

> Everything is in confusion on board. The decks are littered with stores, vegetables, hen-coops, sheep-pens, and coils of rope. There is quite a little crowd of sailors round the capstan in front of the cabin door. Two officers,

with lists before them, are calling over the names of men engaged to make up our complement of hands, and appointing them to their different watches. Though the ship is advertised to sail this evening, the stores are by no means complete. The steward is getting in lots of cases; and what a quantity of pickles! Hens are coming up to fill the hen-coops. More sheep are being brought; there are many on board already; and here comes our milk-cow over the ship's side, gently hoisted up by a rope.

Cows were kept for milk and chickens for eggs, but livestock would also be slaughtered at sea on board the *London* to provide fresh meat.

Passengers ate on board during the stay at Gravesend but, by the afternoon of 30 December, the vessel was ready to set sail. The traditional route took them through the Thames Estuary, southwards down the Kent coast, westwards along the English Channel past the Isle of Wight, and then onwards to Plymouth. The wind got up as the *London* approached the Nore; this sandbank at the entrance to the Thames marked the limits of the ship's cruise on its first sea trial fourteen months before. Captain Martin anchored here and rode out the wild weather for the whole of the next day.

Beyond the Thames

When the wind died down, the anchor was weighed at dawn on New Year's Day 1866, and the *London* steamed into the English Channel against a head wind. The next day, the wind increased as the ship attempted to pass south of the Isle of Wight and further progress became impossible. Lots of the passengers were sick. George Thompson, the pilot, and Captain Martin agreed to seek refuge in the Solent and the ship lay-to overnight while the gale eased. At 10 a.m. on 3 January they resumed their course, passing the Needles Lighthouse on the Isle of Wight at 4 p.m. Passenger James Wilson recorded his impression of the voyage so far:

> By this time we had an opportunity of judging of the sea-going qualities of the *London* and I must say I was very disappointed in her. I could see she was a ship of great length for breadth, heavily sparred, very low in the water, not at all lively or buoyant; and when contemplating the thoughts of her in a gale, I actually entertained fears for her.

The *London* eventually arrived off Plymouth a day late on the 4th, but the going had been laborious, with strong winds, thick rain, and a tremendous sea with a confused swell.

Here a tragic event occurred. The *London* signalled for a local pilot to navigate the vessel to a safe mooring. A cutter came towards them, towing a small boat in which sat a pilot, Joshua Shannon, and his assistant Edward Vettery. There was still a heavy sea running, so the men were towed as close to the ship as possible but, when the tow-rope was let loose a hundred yards or so from the *London*, the boat capsized and the pilot and his assistant were thrown into the sea.

Above: The *London* was chaperoned by tugs into the Thames until ready to use its own engine. (Brodie Collection, La Trobe Picture Collection, State Library of Victoria)

Right: A typical local pilot with a young assistant.

Captain Martin immediately ordered that one of the *London*'s lifeboats be lowered but there was a delay while the lowering apparatus for the lifeboat was got in order; with the state of the sea and the fact that the ship was moving, it took at least twenty-five minutes to reach the men, even though they were only a few hundred yards away. With some difficulty, the pilot's assistant was saved, but twenty-six-year-old Joshua Shannon sank just as his comrade was pulled into the boat and he never resurfaced. All of this, of course, happened in full view of the horrified passengers who were powerless to intervene. Was it a bad omen? Many on board thought so. At best it showed how totally unprepared the *London* and its crew was to deal with an emergency.

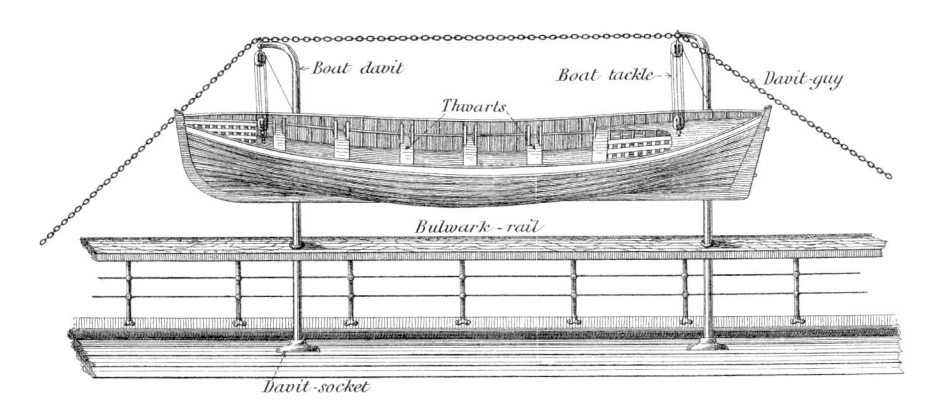

Crews were not well-practised in lowering a ship's boats so response times could be slow.

Two hours later, at around midday, the *London* was successfully at anchor off Plymouth behind the breakwater, which would offer her some protection from any further bad weather. Here an additional fifty-five passengers joined the ship, along with a further load of coal. One young man in Second Class, a Mr Snook, was so unsettled by the 'disastrous' voyage he had encountered thus far that, upon arrival at Plymouth, he immediately disembarked and refused to go any further. His relieved father later reported to the press that

> The side lights [port holes] were less than 24 inches from the water's edge when she left the docks, so that when extra passengers and weight were put on board [at Plymouth] they must have been much nearer. Two of these were broken by the sea going down Channel, literally flooding the tween decks [lower deck], and with several seas breaking over the ship caused her to be more like a floating bath than a passenger ship.
> (*London Evening Standard*, 24 Jan. 1866)

There were other tales of unnamed passengers who did not join the ship at the last moment. It is not clear whether these stories are true, because the individuals are not identified anywhere. For instance, one young man who had fallen out with his family was determined to leave the shores of England for good, or so the story went, but on being discovered on board the *London* he was persuaded by his brother to return home, thus saving his life. A large party of a dozen or more from Cornwall with berths booked on the ship were said to have been so badly held up on their journey to Plymouth that they missed the sailing entirely – something that they regretted bitterly at the time but for which they lived to be grateful.

Survivor James Wilson reveals in his account of the voyage that he knew of at least three passengers who had been so disturbed by the *London*'s poor performance on the voyage to Plymouth that they wanted to leave the ship, but they were afraid of being branded cowards.

Even more unfortunate than these were the four seamen who agreed to join the SS *London* at short notice in Plymouth to replace the six men who had not turned up at East India Docks. However, one seaman, Richard Jones, who had agreed to join the crew in Plymouth got so drunk ashore that he didn't make it on board and, like the other fortunate people who didn't make it to the ship by some twist of fate, he must have been very thankful when he later learned of the *London*'s sinking.

There were other unlucky voyagers on the ship. A lady named Fanny Batchelor had hoped to sail on the SS *London*, but was disappointed to discover there were no berths free. Accordingly, when a cabin became vacant at the last moment, Captain Martin contacted her and invited her to join the ship, which she did. Mr and Mrs Wood and family were similarly ill-starred. They were travelling with three children and two step-children aboard the ship *Victory*. However, when port officials inspected the *Victory*, they ordered the whole family off, as the cabin accommodation was substandard; they took the SS *London* instead. Sadly they all died on the *London*, while their original ship, *Victory*, reached its destination safely.

Perhaps the most unfortunate of all was Alexander Burrell of Glasgow, who had been about to journey to Melbourne with his business partner, John Patrick. Burrell was detained on business at the last moment and so he sent his nine-year-old son, William, in his place. William had not wanted to go without his father. One can only imagine what this poor boy's father went through when he learned the news of the SS *London*'s demise.

While at Plymouth, the *London*'s final point of departure from the UK, the ship had to be visited and signed off as safe by an emigration officer. Consequently, John Stoll came on board and was escorted on a walkabout by Captain Martin and the ship's surgeon, Vivian Faull. Stoll described his examination of the ship in the inquiry that followed the loss of the ship, and his inspection sounds somewhat superficial:

> I did not observe that she had received any injury on her voyage from London to Plymouth, not the slightest. The inspection I made was going round the decks, examining boats, seeing that they had life-buoys [lifebelts], and all that sort of thing, in their places. I took a general view of her rigging and spars, and then I looked round into the engine room, and sent for the chief engineer to speak to him: he reported to me that his department was in perfect order...

So the engine room was fine because the engineer said so; the rigging looked all right at a glance; and there was no damage to the ship because he was not shown any; but at least all the lifeboats and lifebelts were in the right place. The sloping shoulders of Victorian officialdom clearly in evidence.

During their last evening in Plymouth the passengers socialised. James Wilson recalls what would turn out to be a rather chilling conversation:

> In the course of the evening the usual questions were asked, as it generally is at the beginning of a voyage – what is to be the length of time for the

SS *London*. (Wilson P. Evans collection, State Library of Victoria)

passage? And usually bets are made. One would give sixty days ... others would give her sixty-five to seventy days. One man said, 'I'll take odds she never gets to Melbourne. Do you remember what I told you at Gravesend, that she looked like a coffin?' Not a very comforting observation, but I remember it distinctly.

Departing England

Setting sail on a Friday was traditionally regarded as bad luck by sailors – 'Friday sail always fail', as the saying had it. So Captain Martin delayed a short while and weighed anchor a few minutes after midnight on the morning of Saturday 6 January; at this time the weather was calm with only a light northerly wind. He ordered full steam ahead and the ship made good progress at about 8 knots. They sighted the lighthouse on the Lizard, Cornwall, in the early hours of the morning and, at about 6 a.m., the wind veered to the west.

Unfortunately, as the morning of 7 January progressed, the weather began to deteriorate: the wind increased; there were heavy squalls of rain and a head sea arose, buffeting the steamship, slowing progress and making it uncomfortable for the passengers, so that many were sick and kept to their cabins. Some of the coal stored on the main deck broke loose and began rolling around. The *London* ploughed doggedly on, however, and the passengers took comfort from Sunday worship on board the ship. Revd Draper and Dr Woolley jointly led worship in the First Class saloon, and Revd Kerr conducted religious services in Second Class. By noon, the ship was 170 miles from Plymouth. During the day, the *London* passed several other ships that were also making the best of the foul weather, and at this point there was no concern for the safety of the ship. However, passenger

John Munro, who survived the wreck, was surprised to notice that water was coming down one of the hatchways.

The next day, a gale was blowing so Captain Martin stopped the engines and hoisted the *London*'s topsails to move slowly ahead by the power of the wind alone. At noon, the wind lulled somewhat and the captain resumed his engines, steaming slowly ahead for the afternoon and into the night. But the weather changed once more: a gale arose, and at night the large fore-and-aft spanker sail at the stern of the ship was split in two by the wind. Seaman John King, and others, battled with the damaged sail under the direction of Captain Martin and managed to haul it aboard.

Dr John Woolley led worship. (Eugene Scott, artist. Image courtesy of State Library of Victoria)

Heavy weather made the passengers seasick.

During 8 January, John Munro again noted that the main hatchway was not watertight:

> Some heavy seas came down the main hatchway. Soon after tea, we all turned to and carried the water in buckets up the ladders. Nearly all night the ladies were much frightened.

Another passenger, James Wilson noticed the same problem. The access to the Second Class cabins was via the main hatch and it did not seem to close properly so that it leaked. This was made worse by the fact that water seemed to accumulate on the deck above their heads:

> *London* was a very wet ship, much more so than any I had ever seen. Her decks were continually covered with water, more or less swashing from one side to the other; and she had such a wholesale way of taking it in. She would roll well over on her side (and she was a devil for rolling!), and scoop in the green seas, and then it would take ten or fifteen minutes before it would run off.

The reason for this poor drainage became clear when he and other passengers investigated. The scuppers, which were supposed to drain water off the main deck, were very small and blocked up with lumps of coal that had broken loose from the bags on the main deck. He and other passengers attempted to clear them; the next day midshipman Edwards and third officer Angel did the same, but in no time at all they blocked up again because there was so much loose coal around.

All through the night the wind howled and the ship rolled and creaked. The passengers were unable to sleep and sat in their cabins reading, praying and talking. Many of them were nervous. Captain Martin was kept busy all night and it is claimed he never slept from this time until the ship went down; but no-one got much sleep.

The *London* was now well into the Bay of Biscay off the west coast of France, an area notorious for bad weather, but would daylight on the morning of 9 January bring relief from the elements that had plagued the ship since leaving Gravesend?

8

The Sinking

Early on the morning of Tuesday 9 January, about 7 a.m., a heavy sea broke over the poop of the *London* and tore away the port-side lifeboat. Two hours or so later, as the ship continued to press on into the storm, the *London*'s bows suddenly lurched downwards, pitching into the waves as water dramatically submerged the forecastle. When the bows re-emerged, seconds later, the sea had wrought serious damage: the jib boom and flying jib boom had broken away. These were spars used to extend the length of the bowsprit at the front of the ship. Shortly afterwards the tops of the foremast and mainmast followed suit: the foretopmast, fore-topgallantmast, fore-royalmast, and main-royalmast snapped off. This meant that both the bowsprit and the fore mast were now stumps, less than half their original length, and the main mast was also reduced in height.

The damaged masts could not be cleared away properly because the *London*'s iron rigging was difficult to sever. In the midst of a storm, of course, this was even more difficult because the ship plunged and lurched, and the decks were constantly awash. Consequently, portions of the wreckage swung noisily and dangerously with the motion of the ship – the jib boom thumped against the starboard hull and the top of the foremast clattered among the remaining rigging. Passenger John Munro, in particular, was later very critical of this clutter being allowed to stay in situ. The loose coal rattling around, which he had first seen two days ago, was still all over the deck and obstructing the scuppers that should have allowed water to drain away freely, and it was now accompanied by stray spars and casks rattling around as well.

> Thus the men had not even a fair chance to move with any safety about the decks; they were in danger of getting their legs injured or broken by the timber and loose things rolling and washing about.

Munro was a reasonably experienced seafarer himself, having been a sailmaker and rigger at sea for over five years. He was appalled that none of the crew would pay attention to the fact that the hatch covers were not properly battened down, so that water kept pouring into the bowels of the ship. The hatch covers had to be screwed down properly and then covered with a tarpaulin to make them watertight:

> All this time the water was going down all the hatchways, and no-one was trying to stop or check it. There was not a tarpaulin on one of the hatches. I went to Mr Harris and asked him for some tarpaulins, as I could nail them down myself, if I had them; but he said, with reference to the water – 'let it go down'. I then went to the second officer [Arthur Ticehurst], and asked him. He went and brought me an old tarpaulin, a hammer, and some nails, but he sent no-one to help me. I tried to nail the tarpaulin down without assistance, but the ship took in so much water, and rolled so heavily that I was washed across the deck; and I threw down the hammer and nails in despair, and went on to the poop. I went no more to the main deck.

The storm continued, and the unfortunate passengers could do little but huddle in their cabins and the saloons, distracting themselves as best they could by reading and talking while the elements did their worst in the world above their heads. When evening came, after a full day of being tossed and turned, there was little sleep to be had, as the noise and irregular movement of the *London* continued overnight.

Early on the morning of Wednesday 10 January, at around 2 a.m. or 3 a.m., Captain Martin decided that enough was enough. He gave the order to put the ship about, set the engines at full speed, and headed for the safety of Plymouth, where the *London* could escape the storm and be repaired. Survivor James Wilson reported that the passengers by this stage were very afraid: 'All was confusion and terror in our Second Class cabin: ladies clinging to you and beseeching you to stay with them … Most of the men had fear on their faces.' The bad weather continued all day, but the crew did manage to retrieve some of the damaged masts and secure them. The jib boom was hauled aboard and secured to the fore rigging, and the flying jib boom was got in and laid next to the engine room hatch cover, with one end tied down.

The storm deteriorated further as they steamed NNE, heading for safety. The wind howled and the seas were very heavy indeed, swamping the port side of the ship repeatedly. The *London* struggled but its little engine drove the heavy ship doggedly onwards. It was slow and laboured progress but, at this point, most people on board must have assumed that they would make it back home. The ship was damaged but still seaworthy. It was virtually a new vessel, and surely the engines and an experienced captain would see them through.

During the day, more sails were torn away and, as seas continued to crash over the ship, one inundation ripped away the starboard lifeboat and cutter. There were now only four of the *London*'s original boats left intact.

As night fell, passengers huddled together in the dark and everyone was frightened of the ship suddenly going down while they were trapped below

The starboard lifeboat and cutter were torn away by the storm.

decks. The hatch covers were still leaking tremendously and there was water everywhere, as James Wilson relates:

> By seven or eight o'clock we were in as great a state of terror as on the previous night, and with more cause for the gale was more violent ... Imagine what your feelings would be, waiting and expecting every moment to meet death. Add to that, the dismal sound of water rushing in. You ... were not sure whether the ship was filling or not; in fact, a foot or so of water washing to and fro carrying with it every movable article, strengthened your fears that she was. Then at every heavy roll a woman shrieked. There was one young girl nearly frantic. By nine o'clock we were in worse state than ever; when the ship rolled there would be nearly two feet of water in the cabin. It would come in with a rush, then back again to the other side, carrying with it anything that was not lashed.

Then, at about 10.30 p.m., a critical event occurred that changed everything and sealed the fates of almost everyone on board. A mountainous wave towered over the port side of the ship and came crashing down amidships near the *London*'s funnel. To the horror of the men in the engine room, the huge weight of sea smashed open the half-inch plate glass of the engine room hatch cover, so that water and glass cascaded down onto them. Some of the firemen were scalded by the steam as water hit the fires. A passenger and a sailor were washed down as well, but were not badly hurt. When the seas cleared off the deck, the full extent of the damage was clear. The hatch cover was not only smashed open – it had been completely lifted off by the force of the sea. The heavy iron-framed cover was over 12 feet by 9 feet and weighed about a ton and a half, and yet it was no match for the angry Atlantic.

There was now a large hole over the centre of the ship where the hatch cover had been, and it connected all the way down to the lowest reaches of the vessel, which housed the coal-powered fires that drove the ship's engine. Every time a wave broke over the *London*, torrents of water would surge down that opening. The water levels in the engine room rose quickly and very soon reached a depth of a few feet. Once at this height, the cold winter sea gushed greedily into the furnaces via the doors through which the firemen shovelled their coal. Glowing red was quenched to smouldering black in an instant. The ship's fires were out, the engine ceased, and the propeller stopped rotating; the *London* could no longer make headway under its own steam. According to engineer John Greenhill, the ship's fires were extinguished within three minutes of the loss of the hatch cover. Once the seawater reached their chests, the engine-room crew had to abandon their posts.

An initial attempt was made by about twenty men to lift the damaged hatch cover and put it back in place but, soon after they had raised it, the heavy seas caught it, tore it from their hands and smashed it to pieces.

Now began a desperate battle. The crew began to try and cover over the enormous hole on the main deck. They nailed down tarpaulin, stretched sails across the void, used spars and ladders as a framework to replace the hatch cover, even threw beds and mattresses into the hole – anything to try and stem the flow of water. Yet throughout their efforts the *London* continued to pitch and roll; the seas still washed over them and the deck; and the wind tore at whatever coverings they tried to install. Survivors noted that fetching larger sails up from below to stretch over the hole was hampered by cargo or luggage piled up in the passageways.

The failure of propulsion was not necessarily the worst effect of the fires being dowsed; the engines also powered the main pumps, which could have discharged 4,000 gallons of seawater per minute from deep within the ship. Now they were inoperable. The only remaining way to clear the water was to use two small steam-operated pumps on the main deck, which had their own separate boiler and donkey engine. This task was allocated to the third officer, Alfred Angel, and all accounts bear testimony to the diligence and perseverance with which he carried out this duty. These pumps drew away water from the depths of the ship's hold, but cleared far less water than the ship's main pumps (only about 250 gallons per minute).

Sometimes the steam pumps stopped working and had to be operated by hand, and passengers ran to turn the wheels that operated them. Of course water could also be baled out manually by carting it up from the depths of the ship in buckets and throwing it over the side, and this was done for hours on end. By this point, barring some miracle, the *London* was almost certainly doomed. One contemporary author summed up the situation succinctly: 'Her fires out, her sails were useless, and she was but an iron coffin'.

Captain Martin reportedly took the news about the engines calmly, and ordered that the main-topsail be set in an attempt to keep the *London* before the wind. It was important to try and keep the ship moving towards home, and with a sail set the officers could still steer the ship. However, as he no doubt anticipated, the storm ripped it open and shredded it in no time at all with the exception of one corner of canvas. At around this time, he is reported as telling his crew, 'You may say your prayers, boys'.

All through the night, as more and more water poured into the ship, the passengers and crew worked to bale it out from the flooded compartments below and helped to work the pumps. Efforts continued to try and cover over or block the engine hatchway too, but, despite all their hard work, the water gained on them with every minute. John Munro recalled his experience of this gruelling and anxious time:

> The cry was – 'to the pumps'. After being at work some time, I went into the cuddy [dining room]. Two or three ladies were urging the passengers to go and work. It was then (about 3 a.m.) that I particularly noticed Mrs Chapman. She was going about the saloon trying to get volunteers for the pumps, and encouraging all about her to work. I had just come in from a spell at the pumps, when I met her. She asked me to go. She said, cheerfully – 'Come, you're a strong man, go and work.' I told her I had been working for some time, and was tired. She answered that I 'ought not to be tired at such a time'. I went again, well knowing that it was of little or no use; but I could not help going when she asked me. She pressed many more to go, and I never saw or heard one refuse her. She was active and about everywhere, and there were two other ladies about with her: one was Mrs Owen, but I did not learn the name of the other lady. We worked at the pumps and at baling, until everyone saw that it was a hopeless case.

James Wilson went up on deck to help man the pumps in the dark:

> Once on deck, what a sensation it was! Water whirling round you up to the knees – wind piercing cold – night intensely dark. I felt my way along in the darkness, again steadying myself by the ropes etc. on the weather bulwarks, to about midships, to where the pumps were. I could barely distinguish figures in the dark, though I recognised a few voices. It required six to turn the wheels to work the pumps, three at each handle. All were passengers there at the time, excepting two officers, Mr Angel and Mr Grant.

The final death knell came at about 4 or 5 a.m. on Thursday 11 January. With no sails or engines, the *London* kept slewing round with the wind and was later described by surviving passenger David Main as 'like a log in the water'. The ship was low in the sea, heavy, and no longer rose with the waves, but just sat there to be repeatedly pounded and washed over. Being out of control, inevitably there came an occasion when the ship should be stern-side-on when hit by a powerful wave. When this happened, four of the seven stern portholes were smashed open. Since the *London* now sat so deep in the water, it meant the sea could easily enter the vessel via this new series of holes whenever a wave hit the stern. The ship's carpenter tried to rectify the situation by wedging the porthole shutters closed, but they were not watertight and too badly damaged, and so this remedy was partially effective for only a short while until the sea crashed through once more. The furious storm showed no signs of abating and water cascaded into the doomed ship from multiple ports of entry – the four at the stern and the gaping aperture above the engine room – and the lower deck began to flood rapidly.

Many of the male passengers did their best to continue to bail out water and work the pumps, with Dr Woolley, the theologian, and Gustavus Vaughan Brooke, the actor, among them. Brooke was remembered by survivors as exerting particular energy to try and clear away the water, parading the deck bareheaded, barefoot and wearing only a shirt and trousers. Alfred Angel, the third officer, was twenty years old and inexperienced, and yet he manned and supervised the pumps diligently throughout the *London*'s final hours and never left his post. However, survivors noted that many passengers and crew seemed to have given up before this point and simply awaited their fate.

Many of the women, children and exhausted men of all classes huddled together in the saloon to listen to the prayers and heavenly consolations offered by Daniel Draper, who was singled out by survivors as someone who did his best to provide comfort to those who knew they were going to die. Revd Draper had been earnestly leading religious fellowship in the saloon since at least the Wednesday. In a devoutly Christian age, this image of the steadfast preacher urging his fellow travellers to repent and prepare to meet God provoked much praise and satisfaction. But the passengers, it seems, were more determined to be good Christians than survivors: 'the praying paralyzed them', as surviving steward Edward Gardner later remarked. They had a long time to accept that the SS *London* was sinking, and so were prepared to meet their maker and resigned to their fate. There was no stampeding to the ship's boats; no screaming, panic or hysteria.

Revd Draper was heard to call out time and time again: 'O God, may those who are not converted, be converted now – hundreds of them'. Passengers would also approach the minister and ask that he pray with them individually or in a small family group. Draper always obliged.

Four of the stern portholes were driven in.

Daniel Draper preached to passengers and prayed with them.

> Mothers were weeping sadly over the little ones about to be engulfed, and the children, ignorant of their coming death, were pitifully inquiring the cause of so much woe. Friends were taking leave of friends as if preparing for a long journey; others were crouched down with Bibles in their hands, endeavouring to snatch consolation from passages long known, or perhaps long neglected. Incredible, say the survivors, was the composure which, under such circumstances, reigned around.
> (*Western Times*, 17 Jan. 1866)

Captain Martin realised there was little hope of saving the ship, but tried to divert all efforts towards covering the engine-room hatch. Filling the hole was vital to any hope of their preservation. By this time, the engineers had determined that the ship held a depth of about 14 feet of water. In other words the *London* was more than half-filled, and now sat even lower in the stormy sea. They did what they could using sails and anything they could lay their hands on, but the wind and the waves were unrelenting; men were thrown all over the decks by successive inundations and were in serious danger of being washed overboard.

As dawn broke, one of the passengers, James Wilson, asked Captain Martin if he should continue baling out water. The two of them went to the engine room, and then the commander looked at him and replied, 'You may, but I think it is of no use'. They walked back together towards the poop and passed some of the crew:

> We saw some sailors and firemen opening cases of liquor, and some with bottles of brandy in their hands: there were several drunk at this time. The captain said to them, calling some by name, 'Don't do that boys! Don't die cowards!'

Only now did some of the crew turn their attention to abandoning ship. There were four of the ship's boats left, and each of them was provisioned, ready for sea.

The first boat chosen for launch was the *London*'s starboard long-boat, referred to in contemporary accounts as the *London*'s 'pinnace'. This was the largest of the boats and could hold as many as fifty people. The boat was made ready at about 10 a.m., and a few men clambered into it while it was being lowered, including able seaman John King and passenger John Munro. However, in their eagerness to launch as soon as possible, the pinnace was probably lowered too quickly. The boat was made of iron and was not kept level on the way down, so that its bows dipped into the waves; it filled up with water, swamped, and turned over, throwing its occupants into the sea. By some incredible stroke of good fortune, King, Munro and colleagues managed to scramble back on to the deck of the *London*. Some sources suggest that a Dutch seaman was lost during the launch attempt.

At this point, Captain Martin decided he should give a frank assessment of the situation to his passengers. He went to the First Class saloon, where people of all classes had assembled, and announced: 'Ladies, there is no hope for us, I am afraid'. It is doubtful that this news came as a surprise to anyone. Revd Draper replied to the catastrophic news by urging the assembled passengers to more prayers: 'Prepare to meet your God!' The last words heard from Revd Draper by survivors, uttered about an hour before the ship sank were: 'Well, my friends, our Captain tells us there is no hope, but the Great Captain above tells us there is hope that we may all get safe to heaven'.

With the ship constantly inundated with waves, trying to move about the decks was extremely difficult especially at night.

Since the loss of the iron pinnace at 10 a.m., everyone on board seemed to have given up hope of survival. As *The Times* reported, 'the exhausted crew appeared indifferent to their fate'.

By 1 p.m., the *London* was going down fast, and the ship sat ever lower in the water. The depth of water in the engine room was now at 19 feet. The port cutter was made ready on the poop, provisioned, and lowered into the sea. This action seems to have been led by John King and a group of crewmen, although engineer Greenhill stated that the captain had authorised it. Yet, even when all was ready, neither crew nor passengers seemed initially very keen to embark on this small open boat, having seen the grim fate of the pinnace. They shrank back from boarding; the sea was so heavy that people were inclined to prefer the frail shelter of the sinking ship to the dangers of a small open boat amid the raging waters. Passengers continued to sit around praying, reading the Bible, and distracting the children, although some were quietly crying or groaning.

Throughout the various commentaries and reporting of the whole disaster, there is an assumption of the impracticality of women abandoning the ship in the situation in which they found themselves. Women were considered frail and delicate creatures that demanded male protection, and an open boat in a storm was simply not the place for them. Apart from this, the clothing worn by women of the period – voluminous crinoline dresses – was quite inappropriate for any kind of physical effort. It is hard to imagine a woman in these clothes clambering down the side of a ship or leaping overboard into a boat. It would have been completely unthinkable for a woman to hoist her dress up, tear it short or, even worse, remove it, in order to abandon ship, even if it meant saving her life.

The large and bulky crinoline dresses of the period made it almost impossible for women to abandon ship.

One passenger, however, Mrs Owen, told the captain that she and her four-year-old daughter did wish to try and escape via the cutter. Captain Martin was clearly surprised, but was firmly of the opinion that this was not something she should attempt. He told her that she might be exposing herself to a painful and lingering death in an open boat and, as he tried to explain that there was no hope, his calm demeanour finally deserted him, and he broke down and cried. What had he imagined would be Mrs Owen's fate in the cutter? The survivors would need to work desperately to keep the boat afloat and might only endure a few hundred yards before being tipped into the sea; or maybe they would be cast adrift for days – starving, without water, never picked up, and left to die slowly. Either way, this was no place for a lady like Mrs Owen. We now know that all the men who chose the open boat lived to tell their tale, so it seems curious that the captain should dissuade others from even attempting to escape. Yet it has been suggested that, even on the sinking deck of the *London*, he was perhaps more concerned with the propriety of a woman being alone at sea with a group of men, especially since he probably knew the seamen would pack alcohol on the boat. Young Edwards, the midshipman, later recalled the captain saying that he was aware of several drunken seaman who might get into the boat. Whatever his motivation, he succeeded, and Mrs Owen relented. She and her child accepted their fate with the other passengers who stayed on board. Tragically, if Captain Martin had not intervened, or she had kept her resolve, the Owens would have lived.

Gardner, one of the stewards, later related that revolvers were seen in the hands of several passengers, who did not conceal their intention to provide for themselves a quick end when the last moment came. He overheard an offer by the owner of one pistol to his friend that he would shoot him if desired. This was declined at the time but, whether this, or any shooting, took place in the dying seconds of the *London* we will never know. Passenger Wilson had already seen a few bodies floating on the deck by this stage.

Abandoning Ship

Captain Martin spoke to John Greenhill, the second engineer, and gave him his instructions for taking charge of the ship's cutter: 'There is not much chance for the boat; there is none for the ship. Your duty is done; mine is to remain here. Get in and take command of the few it will hold'.

At around this time, as the cutter was being launched, the most famous parting words were uttered, perhaps fittingly, by the actor Gustavus Vaughan Brooke. He spoke to the steward, Edward Gardner, just before he boarded the boat and said, 'If you succeed in saving yourself, give my kind farewell to the people of Melbourne'. These words were repeated often in Australian newspapers over the weeks that followed the tragedy.

Two of the seamen, John King and William Daniels, at work on launching the cutter, urged the ship's boatswain, butcher, cook and a group of others to start work on launching the *London*'s second pinnace at the same time. This was begun, as King and Daniels returned to the cutter.

Gustavus Vaughan Brooke's gentle farewell to Melbourne was remembered long after his death.

Once their boat was in the water, midshipman Edwards thought about joining them:

> I jumped into the port cutter from the mizzen shrouds. I asked King and Daniels would they allow me in, and they said 'Yes', and bid me jump. I did so. The fall was about ten feet. The other midshipman [Robert Clough] was in the next shrouds. He said he was afraid to jump, and he went down with the ship.
> (*The Times*, 6 Feb. 1866)

The *London* was settling down fast and the cutter needed to be away from the ship's side soon to avoid being sucked down into the whirlpool of the sinking wreck. Those who sought the boat as their last chance of survival had to jump from the main deck as young Edwards did; it was a daunting prospect. The passengers had seen the fate of the iron pinnace and were not inclined to take their chances on the even smaller cutter. Passengers John Munro and David Main looked down at the small boat and even they initially decided against it:

> At a little before 2 o'clock, the hour at which the vessel went down, the ladies in an insensible state were floating about on the poop of the ship, and at this time both Mr Munro and Mr Main, looking out upon the little boat that was being tossed like a cockle shell – now close to, and anon 20 yards from the vessel's side – remarked that if they had a chance they would not get into her, believing it impossible for her to live. But, suddenly

they felt the big ship leave as it were their feet, and then it was that they resolved to take chance in the small craft.
(*Otago Times* 23 March 1866)

Having decided to take the cutter, John Munro was sent by the occupants to try and find one last person to join them. He sought out his good friend, John Hickman, and tried to persuade him to take the final vacant seat on the boat. But Hickman was travelling with his wife and four children and obviously could not be persuaded to desert them. John Munro helped his friend move his children to a drier spot because the saloon was now filling with water, then they shook hands, and Hickman said 'Good bye, Jack'. John Munro had to leave his friend forever, but those words must have lingered in his memory for a lifetime.

Since their own situation was perceived to be hopeless, many passengers thought not of themselves, but of those they would leave behind. Some of them wrote messages and cast them into the sea in bottles, hoping that one day they might be found. One young man, John Eastwood, told Munro that he regretted that his father would not now receive the £500 of savings that he had wanted to give him because he would die without leaving a will and so no-one in his family would even know about the money. He broke down in tears as he contemplated his poor father.

However, contrary to initial newspaper reports of the passengers' quiet acceptance of their fate, James Wilson later recalled that some men begged the sailors preparing the boat to be allowed to join them:

> I heard men beseeching of them to let them go, also offering large amounts of money; the answer was 'We don't want your money'. When my friend the sailor gave me permission to go [on the boat], I thought of the ladies and asked myself the question, 'Am I robbing them of any chance they might have?' and said to my friend in the boat: 'Well, I do not like going and leaving those behind', pointing to some that were standing near the mizzen mast. Not that I thought many could be saved, but should like to have a few in the boat, in case we were saved, to show we were not selfish. He said, 'I am as sorry as you, but it can't be helped; try and save yourself'.

Yet there were also many acts of kindness recalled by survivors. Mrs Draper insisted that the seamen in the boat took her blanket to keep themselves warm in the boat. 'But what will you do without it?' one of them asked. 'It will only be for a few minutes longer', she is said to have replied stoically. Mrs Chapman also provided the men with blankets from her cabin.

Meanwhile, John Munro, having failed to persuade his friend to join him in the boat, hunted for a lady who might come instead. He persuaded a young woman to accompany him but, when she reached the ship's side and saw how far she would have to jump, she refused. Munro leapt aboard the cutter himself:

> It was just as she was ready to leave the ship that I jumped into her. It was immediately after, and just before the boat finally left, that I saw

Mrs Chapman looking over, and throwing a parcel of red herrings into the boat; and then she took a railway rug from her shoulders, and pitched it into the boat, saying that 'it would be of some use to us'. King caught it. The blankets and the railway rug proved of great service.

The boat's crew could see Captain Martin on the deck and urged him to join them. 'No', he replied, 'I will go down with the passengers. Your course is E. N. E. to Brest', and, throwing them a compass, 'I wish you God speed, and safe to land'. At the last moment, John Jones the chief engineer got aboard. By this time the sea was so high up the side of the *London* that Jones had hardly any distance to jump.

There were dangerous, deep swirls of water building up around the *London*'s stern. The cutter grated against the larger vessel's side as they were suddenly pushed together and Munro whipped his hand away to avoid being crushed, but caught his ring between the two, and the precious stone it carried was squeezed out. The cutter put off from the ship's side, overloaded with nineteen persons, and they realised they would have to get away immediately to avoid being sucked down with the *London*; they had already tarried for over 45 minutes since launch. As they pulled away strenuously on the oars, it is said that a young woman ran to the side of the ship and promised a thousand guineas if the boat would take her in. This was prominently reported in newspapers, but denied by some survivors, although John Munro later said that a young doctor on board had shouted an offer of £500 from the deck of the sinking ship if they would return to pick him up. Either way, it was simply not possible to row back to the sinking ship at the height of so furious a storm. All the activity to launch the

Pulling away from the stricken ship.

cutter must not obscure the fact that the elements were still raging, and the seas ran dangerously high. The survivors later recounted that they had little hope for their own survival, especially since the boat was carrying seven people more than it was built to carry, and they all thought that they were probably simply prolonging the inevitable.

As the boat got a short distance off, Munro saw Mrs Chapman wave a white handkerchief at them; others waved their caps or cheered. There was a large group of as many as fifty people assembled on the poop. Munro felt that the other passengers were keen for someone to make it back to shore to explain what had happened to them. The steadfast Alfred Angel was still doggedly at his post by the pumps, hoping against hope.

Gerard Moultrie wrote a book about the SS *London* shortly after the news broke that it had been lost. He interviewed many of the survivors, and his account of the great ship's last moments as seen from the boat has a deadly ring of authenticity about it:

> About five minutes afterwards, and when they had got eighty or ninety yards, they looked towards the ship, and saw that she was going down stern foremost. The wind at this time was raging so violently that the men in the boat could not hear each other when eagerly shouting. It was with a kind of dumb wonderment that they saw what transpired. As the ship sunk it was seen that all on deck were driven forward, not by water, but by a tremendous and overpowering rush of air from below, which, as it escaped through the deck as well as the hatches, impelled all on

The SS *London* went down stern first.

deck forward with violence, and their dreadful struggle must have been, therefore, soon over!

In a single moment the men in the boat seemed to take in at a glance all that transpired on board. They saw the stem [bows] of the vessel rise so high, that her keel was completely out of water as far as the foremast. The boatswain, the butcher, the baker, and the purser's mate, it is said, had resolved to attempt their escape in the remaining boat over the cuddy, which was already provisioned and launched; but no sooner were these men ready to put off, than the sinking vessel sank beneath them, making, in her descent, a very whirlpool of angry and confounding water, and the escaping ones in the cutter saw their comrades swallowed up quickly and disappear with the lost ship … For a moment they saw two men with life-belts struggling amid mountains of water: they rose with the waves, and then descended into the deep, deep grave which the sea formed for them, and then not a trace of men or ship was to be seen.

Survivors Adrift

It was a little after 2 p.m. The nineteen occupants of the cutter were all men and they took it in turns to row the boat. There were three passengers – John Munro, James Wilson, and David Main – the rest being crewmen as listed below:

John Jones, chief engineer
John Greenhill, second engineer
John Armour, third engineer
Thomas Brown, fireman
Walter Edwards, midshipman
Daniel Smith, boatswain's mate
William Hart, carpenter's mate
Edward Gardner, second class steward
William Daniels, quartermaster
John King, able seaman
Benjamin Sheals, able seaman
Richard Lewis, able seaman
James Gough, able seaman
Edward Quin, able seaman
William Crines, seaman
Alfred White, ship's boy

The cutter sat low in the water and was carrying too many people. It was resolved that everyone should stay exactly where they were, since any moving about on the boat was liable to upset it. One account suggests that, as the ship was going down, the seamen were concerned about survivors from the wreck attempting to clamber on board. This would certainly have capsized the boat, and some of them, it is said, drew knives in preparation for warding off any such attempts.

The cutter was now alone in the dangerous waters of the Bay of Biscay, in a storm, and a long way from the nearest landfall, Brest, on the coast of France. The boat had no sails and the best way to keep it afloat was to keep running before the wind because, although this set them heading away from Brest, it was the only way to limit the amount of sea breaking over the boat. King wisely advised them all to put the dreadful fate of the *London* out of their minds, and concentrate on working together for survival. Daniel Smith was initially given the task of steering; there was no tiller so he had to use his bare hands to manoeuvre the rudder and they were soon frozen. After three hours he gave way to John King, and fortunately for everyone on board he proved highly capable. They hoped for survival, but everyone on board was soon cold, wet, hungry, thirsty and very fatigued. They had to bail out several times with tin cans and a bucket whenever seas broke over them. The blankets proved invaluable; Munro even tore up one of them to make hats for those who did not have any. The boat had been hastily provisioned and there was only a quart of water on board, but this was ruined by seawater and had to be thrown overboard. There was, however, a large bag of biscuits, some carrots and some turnips. Young Edwards, the midshipman, realised that among the provisions were two bottles of brandy and some champagne. He managed to hide one of the bottles out of fear that the seamen would get drunk and ruin their chances of survival, but the rest was shared out as vital sustenance.

The survivors had not been afloat two hours before they saw a sailing ship race past them, but it was at too great a distance to hail.

At about midnight the wind eased off somewhat, but initially it was so dark that the occupants of the boat could not even see each other. The conditions continued to improve, but at about 3 a.m. on Friday morning a wave curled right over the boat and swamped it, and they had to bail out furiously. This was dangerous work because hasty movement about the boat was liable to turn it over; they had to be careful. It was January, and the sea was freezing cold, so this drenching was potentially life-threatening; it had certainly reduced the length of time they could sit in the boat without fear of dying from exposure. The young teenagers, Walter Edwards and Alfred White, were at particular risk.

The skies began to clear a little and, shortly after this, they saw hope: a ship close at hand, lit up by feeble moonlight, and they hailed her; however, although they were heard by the vessel's crew, the survivors could not make themselves seen. The boat was very low in the water; the sea was still running high; and they had no light to show in the darkness. The mysterious ship set about searching for them, but eventually they became separated. It must have been a most dispiriting moment.

However, at about 9 a.m., they sighted two more ships – a barque to starboard and a schooner to port. The confused cross seas made it very difficult for the cutter to reach either of them, but they made for the ship on their starboard bow. John King was initially reluctant to steer for either ship, because it meant turning across the wind and this risked the boat being swamped, but the other survivors were so afraid that one of them threatened to stave the boat in if he wouldn't alter course. He did so, and they hoisted an old shirt on an oar and waved it to attract attention. The barque's crew spotted them and waved their hats in recognition; the vessel hoved to, awaiting them and, after a lengthy period of exhausting rowing, two men to each oar, they almost made the side of the vessel. But then, as John King predicted and within 20 yards of safety, the cutter was suddenly swamped nearly to capacity by a large icy wave that broke over them. Once again they had to bail out desperately, without upsetting their precarious craft. They must have been chilled to the bone, but they survived and eventually made it close enough to the ship so that a line could be thrown down to them. Then they scrambled up the ship's side as best they could.

Their saviour was an Italian barque named the *Marianople*, bound from Constantinople with a cargo of wheat, and under the command of Captain Gion Batta Cavasa 'a fine, jolly, and burly old fellow with a most benevolent countenance'. The men clambered aboard at about noon on Friday 12 January after more than twenty hours afloat in treacherous and wintry conditions. The ship's master spoke little English, but exerted every kindness; the survivors were given a glass of gin, then fresh dry clothes,

The *Marianople* was a cargo ship of the type known as a barque.

hot tea, biscuits, and were allowed to sleep. He even killed some chickens on board so that they might have the pleasure of a satisfying meaty stew. Survivor James Wilson recalled their sudden realisation that they had survived against all the odds:

> We could talk freely, and began to realize more fully the dreadful catastrophe we had witnessed. It appeared more terrible to us now than at the time, or during the night, as our own safety then was very doubtful. In the afternoon I laid down and had a sleep, and a troubled sleep it was. I passed through all the horrors of another shipwreck. And for many nights after, and I may say many weeks after, I had to go through the same ordeal. At night, I can't say we went to bed: most of us lay down on the wheat, which was loose in bulk, and covered ourselves with sails, and felt very comfortable. Such a happy change from last night.

Only later did they learn that the gale had already posed the *Marianople* many problems – in order to withstand the elements, Captain Cavasa had had to jettison part of his cargo. The *Marianople* headed for Falmouth but the rough weather persisted for part of the journey and succeeded in carrying away the ship's rudder. The ship now needed urgent repairs and the captain was pleased to have some extra men on board to help him work and repair the damaged vessel. The *Marianople* docked at Falmouth on Tuesday 16 January, where the grateful survivors thanked their rescuers and were discharged to English soil. Here, they reported their sorry news to the port authorities, who telegraphed the details to London; the next day they hastened to the capital, where they arrived around twenty-four hours later.

Immediately on landing, John Munro scribbled a short letter to his parents in Scotland:

> Dear Father and Mother,
> I have just arrived here, being one of nineteen saved from the foundering of the *London* in the Bay of Biscay. There are 300 drowned in her, I think; but the full particulars will appear in the papers tomorrow. I can say very little, for I have been in a dream for the last three weeks. I don't know what I have been doing, for I have been wet all this time and hungry. I have lost all I have got, and am here in rags. I will try to come to Scotland as soon as I can. All I can say is that I thank God for His goodness to me through all my trials, for I have had many lately. My respects to all inquiring friends.
> I remain your loving son,
> John Munro
> (*Montrose, Arbroath and Brechin Review*, 19 Jan. 1866)

The survivors had worked together to escape death, but a special debt was owed to Able Seaman John King. He had expertly steered the boat through most of their time afloat, dodging the heavy seas. His skill had avoided them being fatally swamped; he had taken a leadership role on the boat;

Able seaman John King.

and eventually enabled them to reach the side of the *Marianople* in safety. He had also been instrumental in launching the cutter in the first place. He managed all this despite being injured on the deck of the *London* at the height of the storm, when he was thrown violently against the ship, cutting his thigh and badly bruising himself.

The tragic story that the survivors told of the loss of the SS *London* and of their own remarkable escape soon raced like wildfire through an incredulous population.

9
The Public Reaction

The initial public reaction to the loss of the robust and high-profile SS *London* consisted of an understandable grief, but mixed with disbelief. How could this possibly have happened to a luxury liner so close to home? The number of dead was uncertain and quoted figures initially varied widely. In fact, at least 243 people had died – 167 passengers and seventy-six crew – although the precise figure may never be known (see Appendix 1). Even the press struggled to break the news:

> Many years have elapsed since we have had to record a disaster at sea so terrible in its details, and involving so wholesale a sacrifice of life as that which we have today to announce.
> (*Western Times*, 17 Jan. 1866)

> A profound sensation prevailed among all circles in the City yesterday morning upon receipt of the sad intelligence that Messrs Money Wigram & Sons' magnificent auxiliary screw steamship, the *London*, had foundered in the bay of Biscay, with upwards of 200 souls on board.
> (*The Times*, 18 Jan. 1866)

> The foundering of the *London*, even as told in the brief recital of the telegrams, was an occurrence to touch the entire nation to the heart; but the details which have since become known are so affecting, so mournful … that the loss will ever be classed among the most famous calamities at sea.
> [*Daily Telegraph*, 19 Jan. 1866]

In recalling public reaction a few weeks afterwards, author Gerard Moultrie wrote:

> At first many positively refused to credit the intelligence that the noble vessel, which had only a few days left our shores, had succumbed to the fury of the gale, and gone down a wreck. It seemed impossible … All were slow to admit that there was no hope, and there was a general clinging to the expectation that there had been some mistake.

JANUARY 17, 1866.

APPALLING SHIPWRECK.

FOUNDERING OF AN AUSTRALIAN STEAMER FROM PLYMOUTH.

LOSS OF TWO HUNDRED AND SEVENTY LIVES.

Many years have elapsed since we have had to record a disaster at sea so terrible in its details, and involving so wholesale a sacrifice of life as that which we have to-day to announce. The event will appear the more appalling to our readers from the fact that a brief ten days ago every one of that ill-fated band of men, women, and children, whose corpses now lie far down beneath the ocean wave, were living, active, hopeful, and were gazing on the hills that shut in the Plymouth Sound. Intelligence reached Falmouth yesterday that the fine Australian passenger vessel, the London, foundered at sea on Thursday last, and that of her crew and passengers, 289 all told, the only survivors, nineteen in number, had landed at the westernmost Channel port. The particulars of the occurrence, as gained from the few who have been left to tell the tale we proceed to give.

The *Western Times* broke the news after getting the first interviews with survivors at Falmouth.

Yet in many ways it was even worse for those waiting anxiously for loved ones on the other side of the world. In the days before modern communications, the terrible news of the *London*'s fate took two months to reach Australia, and eventually arrived via a mail ship on 15 March 1866. A special edition of Melbourne newspaper *The Argus* was printed to report the awful event that it described as falling like a thunderbolt on its community. Until then, the inhabitants of Australia had been blissfully unaware that their dear friends or family members had been dead since 11 January, something that must have been very hard to accept. The citizens of Melbourne were especially distraught because so many people on board had lived locally or had connections with the city; the anonymously authored *Sorrow on the Sea* captures the feelings that prevailed:

> A grief of no common magnitude has fallen on this city and land. The steamer that brought the January mails to us brought with them a 'freight of woe'. The burden of the brief and terrible tale was that the steamship *London* had foundered in the Bay of Biscay, with 270 souls on board. As the appalling tidings spread with electric speed, business came almost to a dead stand, men gathered in groups at the corners of the streets, the most painful anxiety and suspense were exhibited, and the city became shrouded in gloom … The chasm opened in many a family circle is so

wide and saddening, that it was scarcely to be wondered at that the tidings should penetrate with a great and sudden grief every relation of life and all the ramifications of society, and that men should stand awe-stricken in the presence of the fearful calamity.

People lingered anxiously at the Exchange in Melbourne for any further news by electric telegraph, and went to the newspaper office, desperate for more information. As in the UK, there was initial disbelief, but all local people could do was wait. Shops closed as a mark of respect, and in many of their windows was displayed Gustavus Vaughan Brooke's last words: 'Give my kind farewell to the people of Melbourne'.

However, the relatives and friends of the people on board the *London* were not the only ones who had cause to mourn deaths at sea. The storms had swept over a wide area and claimed many other victims:

The 11th of the present January will long be remembered in many English homes now desolate. The nation awoke that morning to find that a storm, unequalled in violence for the last fifty years, had swept over the western coast of Europe. Inland, the whole system of telegraphy in the southern part of the British Isles had been destroyed. At sea, from every point of the compass, came intelligence of disaster and loss of life. In Torbay alone,

The Exchange in Melbourne where local people gathered waiting anxiously for more information. (State Library of Victoria)

between thirty and forty vessels alone had been lost, and property to the amount of a quarter of a million of money destroyed.
(*Huddersfield Chronicle*, 27 Jan. 1866)

The storms had been very severe. On 25 January, *The Times* reported that the Board of Trade had collected testimonies from over 400 captains and witnesses to try and ascertain the total extent of the losses at sea. Its report lists numerous named vessels lost or severely damaged by the weather in early January, including this small selection:

- *Old Honesty*, barque, of Dundee, struck on the Goodwin sands; ship lost.
- *Jessy*, brig, of Exeter, driven against the cliffs at Brixham; ship and five lives lost.
- The brig *Brothers*, of North Shields, abandoned at sea in a sinking state.
- *Bessie*, steamer, wrecked on the Letant Sand; crew taken off by lifeboat; ship lost.
- *Mary Winch*, brig, of Hartlepool, driven ashore and became a total wreck.
- *Volunteer*, from New Brunswick, disappeared in the storm with all hands and never seen again.
- The ship *Medina* of North Shields, run down by a steamship and sunk.
- *Monda* from London, driven on rocks near Brixham Harbour and five lives and the ship lost.

The total losses during the gales were reported as the most numerous that had happened off the coast of Britain since February 1838.

When the terrible news of the *London*'s demise broke, the public had only recently read of another maritime tragedy as well – the loss of the lifeboat at Gorleston, near Yarmouth in East Anglia. On 13 January the crew of the lifeboat *Rescuer* had set out to attend a vessel flying a signal of distress, but their boat was flipped over by a heavy sea, and twelve of the crew drowned. This was a disaster – yet the vessel involved was a small open boat and not a large and powerful steamship.

One passenger ship, the 3,000-ton steamship *Amalia*, was actually wrecked in the vicinity of the SS *London* during the same storm in the Bay of Biscay. It too carried emigrants and a valuable cargo, and was bound initially for Malta and Alexandria under Captain Perius. The *Amalia* had three lifeboats destroyed during the storm on 10 January and, like the *London*, the ship lost the power of its engines when hatches on the main deck were carried away and the engine room flooded. However, the passengers and crew of this vessel were more fortunate than those aboard the *London* because, when the *Amalia*'s condition became critical, there was another vessel within hailing distance – the *Laconia* – that took everyone off the stricken ship. They stood on deck and watched the SS *Amalia* sink before being ferried home to safety. Whatever the circumstances or similarities, the fact that everyone on board the *Amalia* survived made the loss of the *London* all the more inexplicable.

Notwithstanding all these disasters, many other large vessels had withstood the storm. The survivors of the *London* had seen at least four ships themselves while hoping to be rescued, including the *Marianople*, and then there was the *Laconia* described above. The P&O ship SS *Euxine* had been within 50 miles of the *London* when it sank but sustained no significant damage. Another vessel that weathered all that the Atlantic threw at it was the barque *Susan Pardew*, which was in the Bay of Biscay at the same time as the *London*. This 378-ton wooden ship from Plymouth was a cargo vessel sailing from the Mediterranean under the command of Captain John Davis, and it survived the Biscay storm unscathed. Why had this smaller and technologically inferior ship, and so many others, survived the storms without the great loss of life that the *London* suffered? It was a question asked repeatedly, even during the earliest media coverage of the events. Was the *London* mismanaged, or was it badly designed?

Gloom and disbelief was quickly submerged in some quarters with a kind of quiet gratification that the passengers and crew had at least died bravely as befitted British citizens, and as good Christians: praying, reading the Bible, repentant, and ready to meet the Almighty.

> The curt and bitter intelligence which carried desolation to many a home, now that fuller information has been gleaned from the few who have survived of all on board the stricken ship, may be tempered by the knowledge of how those many encountered their fate – of a rich heroism, and grave, patient, religious submission supervening on the failure of their brave efforts, when all human power was broken down, that will take its place beside other like stories of which the nation is proud.
> (*Daily Telegraph*, 18 Jan. 1866)

The gallant Captain Martin had gone down with his ship, too, and this was considered entirely appropriate and proper: 'Nothing could be finer and nobler than the example set by him to all on board'. In fact, this sentiment went some way towards explaining why commentators were reluctant, at least initially, to look too closely into Captain Martin's behaviour and offer any criticism.

Even where there was fault, the issue was clearly the hubris of humankind in believing that *Homo sapiens* could master the forces of nature. An anonymous book published in Melbourne entitled *The Loss of the Steamship 'London'* suggested that everyone needed a timely reminder of human humility before mightier powers:

> Modern achievements in science have bred and encouraged a vanity and self-complacency which almost seem to necessitate some stupendous catastrophe, that humanity may be reminded how frail and helpless it really is. Of late, nothing has seemed impossible for man to encompass.

The storm might at will be avoided or braved, the raging ocean might batter the strong ship with all its violence, but its fury would be vainly spent against her well-riveted armour ... Science indeed had conquered sky and sea, and divested them of terrors.

That old enemy of the Church – science – could actually be held up by some Christians as being to blame, or at least it could be weakened as the icon of the industrial age:

When reading the particulars of the occurrence, one cannot avoid being impressed with the idea that science, so far from having effected everything to protect and defend the vessel in such an emergency as overtook it, had actually left her helpless. Her iron masts cracked like reeds, and her iron rigging prevented her being cleared of the wreck ... Her iron hatchway, built with the express object of protecting her engines, instead of fulfilling such design, really seems to have invited disaster.

Men of science will tell us that we are conquering nature, and that we can do now without God's love and care. But put these 'wizards that peep and mutter', the setting up of science against God, on the deck of the *London*, in the presence of the hurricane roaring like a wild beast ... Let science stand there and be tried, and it will be found that the Wesleyan preacher who so bravely did his best to lead those who were about to perish with himself to prayer and to God, was a wiser man and a truer hero than any unbelieving man of science who has ever breathed.

Whatever the angle that individual commentators and reporters pursued, there was a genuine outpouring of national distress, and shocked people across the country wanted to do something to comfort the victims' families. As a result, soon after the disaster, on 23 January, a group of gentlemen obtained an interview with the Lord Mayor of London at the Mansion House. They hoped to secure his interest in raising a fund of donations to support the distressed families of crew and passengers who had been bereaved by the ship's loss. Among the deputation was survivor John King, who 'was treated with great respect by all present'. The Mayor listened to the group's proposal and, addressing the deputation, said,

I think it is scarcely necessary for me as Chief Magistrate to say that in common with, I may say, the civilised world, I deeply deplore this great calamity; not only in consideration of those who have been called away and are now beyond our sympathy, but of those who are left behind ... I shall be happy to assist these unhappy persons either by my purse, in my person, or by my position.
(*The Times*, 24 Jan. 1866)

The Mayor himself immediately gave a personal gift of £21, and the fund was formally created. Several banks agreed to act as receivers of the nation's donations at no charge. This was some small comfort for the wives,

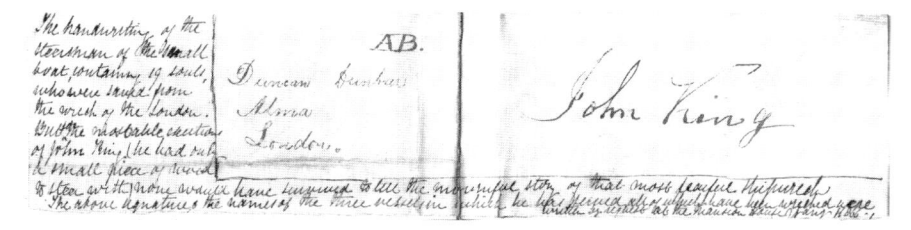

After his meeting with the Mayor of London, John King realised he had become a celebrity; admirers asked him for his autograph and to write down the names of the three ships in which he had been wrecked.

children, and ageing parents, who might otherwise have been thrown into immediate poverty in the midst of their bereavement because their main breadwinner had died.

When it later emerged that John King himself had lost everything in the wreck and had only two shillings to his name, a newspaper campaign helped to raise about £100 to support and reward him.

Reactions from Families

The reaction of individuals to the loss of their loved ones is not well-documented. The tragic sinking of the SS *London* occurred at a time when the media were much more respectful of the privacy that the bereaved need at times of great personal loss. However, the reflections and individual experiences of some of those affected has come to light.

One of the most heartrending accounts concerns Henry Samuel Chapman, the husband of the kindly Catharine Chapman who was mentioned by many survivors as being so considerate to others. Henry was a judge in Dunedin, New Zealand, and had awaited the return of his wife, sons and daughter from England with great anticipation. He was deeply in love with Catherine, whom he always called Kate, and later said their marriage had been one of 'unabated happiness', describing her dotingly as 'faultless'. A local newspaper recounted his reaction to the news:

> Mr Justice Chapman, anxious for information as to his wife, son, and daughter, arrived at the Telegraph Office before ten o'clock. A message from the Bluff was at once handed to him and, after doing little more than glancing at it, he staggered and fell moaning to the ground. The message announced the loss of all those dear to him, who had taken passage on the *London*.
>
> His Honor was raised and attended to by those in waiting at the office, and a medical man was speedily fetched. His Honor slightly rallied, and was then conveyed home.
>
> The sitting of the Supreme Court was adjourned by Mr Justice Richmond as soon as he received the melancholy news.
>
> (*Otago Daily Times*, 23 March 1866)

Henry Chapman lost his wife and three children in the SS *London* disaster. (State Library of Victoria)

Poor Henry Chapman was heartbroken, and the pain of losing three children and his dear wife left him in inconsolable, abject misery. A few weeks later he wrote to his aunts about the disaster that had utterly desolated his happy home:

> Surely no heavier affliction ever fell on man; and it fell all the more heavily from my naturally sanguine, hopeful and buoyant nature. I never could anticipate evil. For months past I have been building up an imaginary palace of domestic happiness derived from the anticipated return of the best of wives, the most promising of sons, the most cheerful, affectionate and idolized of daughters, and my poor little Watty ...
>
> In the little discouragements, annoyances and disappointments inseparable from a very active professional and political life, I never heard even an uncheerful word pass my dear Kate's lips. Her perfect temper, her wonderful equanimity and her calm resolution sustained and comforted me always. All our little troubles (and they were very few) were <u>outside</u> of our happy home: <u>within</u> all was peace. I never met with any human being in whom unselfishness was so completely personified as in my wife. She was the light of our dwelling and the ornament of the society in which we moved.

Reactions like this, though painful to read, do help to remind us that the tragedy of the SS *London* was a human event. Real people died. More than 150 years after the event, Chapman's tender words can still clutch at our hearts and cause us to pity him as he tried to come to terms with such a profound and agonising loss.

Another account of a personal reaction has also survived. In our modern world, all news – good or bad – can be transmitted immediately at the press of a button. These days we have become accustomed to receiving accurate and speedy details after a newsworthy event. Notwithstanding the fact that the unfortunate relatives and friends of the dead had to wait two months for the news in Australia or New Zealand, even in the UK the news did not come quickly by modern standards and Victorian newspapers were often inaccurate. Consequently, many readers with friends or relatives on board the SS *London* doubted the accuracy of what they read, and were determined to find out more for themselves. And so it was that Edward Hingston, theatrical agent to Gustavus Vaughan Brooke, recounts the manner in which the actor's wife, a fellow thespian known professionally as Miss Avonia Jones, learned the news of her husband's death. Hingston described all that happened in a letter he sent to a friend:

> On the morning of the 17th, I was reading the *Daily Telegraph* at breakfast when the telegraphic report of the catastrophe caught my eye. I hastened to Miss Jones's, and waited for some time before I knocked, hoping that she would have seen the intelligence and recovered from the first shock Though the papers were on the table before her, she had not noticed the paragraph. You will understand the position I was in, and how nervous I felt in having to break the news. Told it had to be, and told it was.
>
> The hope which I tried to inspire was that the telegraph had exaggerated facts, and that all were not lost who were stated to have perished. So we took a coach to Money Wigram and Co. in Leadenhall Street – Avonia not speaking a word during the drive. 'It is quite true. Don't have any doubt about it – we have none – they are all lost', said an old man from behind the desk; the office being filled with weeping women and tearful-eyed men.
>
> We found that if we went to the yard at Blackwall we might possibly learn further. On arriving there, no-one could inform us of more than had appeared in the papers. The chance was that, if we could see Greenhill, the engineer who had escaped, we might be further informed, so we drove to his residence in a dreary street of mean houses in the middle of the Isle of Dogs. He had been taken out by some anxious enquirer, and we were forced to return without further news.
>
> On the next day came more accurate reports, depriving us of the faintest gleam of hope, and too sadly corroborating the story of the day before.
> (*The Press*, 18 Apr. 1866)

In a tragi-comic continuation of Gustavus Vaughan Brooke's dissolute reputation before he died, his poor wife was immediately beset by rumours that her husband had sought passage on the SS *London* to elope with another woman. These rumours reached such a fever pitch that Avonia felt obliged to write to *The Times* to dispel the 'malicious reports which have been circulated' and which, she said, were traducing his memory. The same copy of this newspaper, however, and subsequent editions, show that Avonia continued to appear that same night and every night in her successful stage production of *East Lynne* by John Oxenford at the New Surrey Theatre. In the true spirit of the old actors' adage there was no room for private grief: 'the show must go on'.

One final, tragic, personal yet public reaction to the loss of the SS *London* must also be recorded. Elizabeth Marks had taken a Second Class cabin on

Actress Avonia Jones was the wife of Gustavus Vaughan Brooke.

board the ship and, on learning of the death of this dearly beloved younger sibling, her sister Sarah Marks was so heartbroken that she committed suicide. The *Daily News* in London reported this sorrowful incident:

DISTRESSING SUICIDE THROUGH THE LOSS OF THE 'LONDON'
Yesterday Mr William Payne, coroner for the City, held an inquiry at the Golden Axe Tavern, St Mary-axe, relative to the death of Miss Sarah Marks, aged 43 years, who committed suicide by poison through grief, caused by the loss of a sister, 23 years of age, on board the ship *London*. Jacob Hartmann, 19, a boarding house keeper, said that the deceased came to live at his place on Monday week. She had been, witness understood, in business as a linen draper, but had failed. Until last Wednesday, however, she was in good health and spirits, but on that day she heard of the loss of the *London*, and she then became quite frantic. She said that her young sister was lost on board that ship, and that it was she who had persuaded her to go to Australia. She said, 'I am my sister's murderer,' and got almost beside herself. She had also written on a piece of paper, which was found after her death, that she had destroyed herself, for she was the cause of her sister's death by persuading her to go to Melbourne in the *London*. The jury returned a verdict 'that the deceased committed suicide by taking poison while in a state of unsound mind.'
(*Daily News*, 24 Jan. 1866)

The financial needs of many families soon became uppermost in their minds after the initial shock of losing a loved one. Without a corpse to bury, there could be no death certificate; and so families were unable to complete probate on behalf of the deceased individual. This was a common problem in the nineteenth century; no matter how desperate their circumstances, families could not inherit until death had been proved, and this might take years if there was no body. The midshipman, Walter Edwards, and John Munro, the passenger, were communicated with by the Melbourne solicitors of several families to determine if they were willing to help. They were both keen to assist where they could, and so Edwards and Munro agreed to receive photographs of the victims from Melbourne and they were able to positively identify many of them. Munro also remembered the young man who cried on the deck of the sinking *London* because his impoverished father would be denied his son's savings. Munro sought out that father and gave testimony to ensure that he would inherit it.

Meanwhile, survivor James Wilson, though keen to help, was vexed and upset by the attentions he received from others. He wrote to his mother on 20 January:

My dear Mother,
No doubt you will be surprised to hear from me again in England. The steamship *London* is lost: gone to the bottom in the Bay of Biscay, and myself and two others are the only survivors out of 180 passengers! The ship foundered six days after leaving Plymouth, and out of 250 passengers and crew, but 19 are left to tell the tale. The scene was most fearful and heartrending, and one never to be effaced from my memory …

I have suffered considerably from exposure, fatigue, and the consequent mental reaction, but am recovering and I think would soon be quite well again if I could only get rest; but that is almost impossible. The calamity is causing a profound sensation, and letters are pouring in to me from all parts of the kingdom, and persons are calling at all hours inquiring for lost friends and relatives. Some of those meetings are severely trying to my feelings: when persons ask for Mr, Mrs or Miss So-and-so, their brother or sister whom I well knew, had talked with and consoled them as best I could, and bade them good-bye for the last time fully expecting then myself to go down with the ship.

I know that at that dreadful moment my own most painful sensations were to think I should never again behold the loved ones at home, or ever again re-visit the happy scenes of my childhood. None but those similarly circumstanced can know the intensity of those sensations. But when every hope had fled, a merciful Providence provided a means of escape, and I trust we may all meet again.

I could write enough to fill a book, but for the present must say good-bye.
Yours affectionately,
James E. Wilson
(*Morning Chronicle* (Halifax), 1866)

However, many of the families of victims, some of the survivors, and various commentators on events, were desperate for information. They felt that there was blame somewhere for the loss of the SS *London*, and they were determined to root it out. One such was Edward Gilbert Highton, who lost his brother-in-law, Henry Dennis, in the disaster. Highton was a barrister and pamphleteer, and his concerns were soon to raise significant tensions between him and the Victorian establishment; but he wasn't the only one. Sir John Pakington, Conservative MP for Droitwich, was a powerful ally.

Criticism Begins

Concerns began to be expressed about the causes of the loss of the SS *London* almost as soon as the public and the press had recovered from the initial shock. Newspapers were filled with coverage and comment for weeks.

If old wooden ships like the *Susan Pardew* and the *Marianople* had survived the same storms in the same location as the more modern SS *London*, then surely there was fault somewhere. Perhaps it was carrying too much cargo and so was unable to meet the challenge of the storm. In the press, witnesses remarked that the SS *London* was sitting too low in the water when she left port. And wasn't there a huge dead-weight of railway iron that must have affected the ship's ability to weather the storm? The greed of shipowners to carry as much cargo as possible meant that coal had had to be stored on deck to rattle around the decks and block the scuppers that drained water off the main deck. Was this a factor that contributed to the ship's loss? The Australian press was even more critical than the British. The *Sydney Morning Herald* carried this angry editorial on 17 March:

> So far as we can see, the passengers were as much sacrificed by the act of man as they would have been had the ship been run ashore or scuttled at sea. The merchants, who are responsible, are men of reputation ... They insure the ship and its freight. If these go to the bottom they are safe, and are able to purchase more; and if the gambling with the lives of men be successful, then they may net several hundreds by lading their ships to the water's edge. They can give the captain's widow a five-pound note to make up her loss. And what is murder?
>
> We wonder if the consciences of men who do such things ever dream at night. Do they see the victims of their covetousness – like the long procession of assassinated kings in Macbeth – march past their troubled couches?

Besides accusations of being overladen, the ship's design was open to criticism. The *London* was surely too long and narrow to be able to cope well with persistent heavy weather, and the ship was 'over-masted' for its size and shape: it carried far too many sails. Why was it that the engine-hatch cover was carried away? This must have been a design fault. If Lloyd's had assessed the ship and passed it as seaworthy, was there something wrong with their assessment methods? Were they out of date or were their agents too cursory? The ship's iron masts and rigging also meant that

The Walter Edwards' model bows-on: was the SS *London* 'too narrow' for her length?

they couldn't be cut away quickly when they became damaged during the early part of the storm. Had this affected the behaviour of the ship in the prevailing conditions, and its handling?

What about the captain? If he was driven by commercial necessity to make a quick run to Australia, had this made him behave rashly? Had the barometers at Plymouth predicted a storm when the *London* set sail? If so, Captain Martin should have delayed sailing. Yet once the storm started, he could have turned around a lot sooner and retreated to Plymouth. And when, at the height of the storm, he made the fatal decision to turn around and run for home, surely he had simply set the *London* heading back into the eye of the storm through which he had just passed? Or maybe he should have taken in all sail and just hove-to to sit it out? Everyone had a view.

It was often recommended that the topmost parts of each mast – the topgallant masts – be lowered onto the deck when bad weather was imminent to reduce the surface area of ship exposed to the storm. Why had Captain Martin not done this? Storm damage had hampered the *London*'s sailing ability. Had he set proper storm sails that were more resistant to the wind's action than conventional canvas?

Should passengers and crew have exerted more effort to save themselves? They seem to have given up hope too quickly. Could they not have built rafts? Why did they leave it so late to launch lifeboats? Why didn't they launch more? Nearly all the survivors were members of the crew: had they focused on looking after themselves, rather than protecting the passengers? Had the ship's officers done enough to provide leadership during the crisis? Had they and the captain given up too easily?

A good daub of Victorian xenophobia came into the debate too. After all, at least fifteen of the seamen were foreigners, and therefore not as capable as their British counterparts; inclined to be lazy and unable to speak English properly, these men were to blame!

Newspaper editorials, columnists, and letter writers were sure there was something amiss here, but no-one could agree what the main problem was. There were floods of letters, interviews with survivors, and detailed commentaries. Everyone had their theories. The only thing that most people agreed was that the disaster should not have happened, and that steps should be taken to get to the bottom of it. An explanation was needed. Was it the owners' fault? The designers, the captain, the crew? The idea of an inquiry was soon mooted, but it needed to get under way quickly while sufficient survivors were available to be called as witnesses.

Messages from the Dead

In early February 1866 the Commissary-General of Marine at Lorient, Brittany, was informed that various items connected with the SS *London* had been washed up on French shores that overlooked the ship's last resting place in the Bay of Biscay. These included six messages from passengers sealed into bottles. He sent the details to Sir Anthony Perrier, the British Consul at Brest, who passed them on to Admiral Halsted the secretary of Lloyd's underwriters. The Admiral decided it was in the public interest to release the Commissary-General's communication to the press so that relatives and wreck investigators would have access to the information. The letter, translated from the French, is as follows:

> On the 12th of February last three bottles were found on the coasts of Quiberon and Locmariaquer, containing six papers written in English, as follows: -
> **The first paper.** – 'D. W. LEMMON. – London, Thursday 10th January, 1866. The ship is sinking; no hope of being saved. Dear parents, may God bless you, as also me, with the hope of eternal salvation.'
> **Second paper.** – 'Steamship London – they are putting out the boats.'
> **Third paper.** – 'F. G. HUCKSTEPP. – On board the steamship London, lat. 46 deg. 20 min., long. 7 deg. 30 min.; lost boats, masts, and sails; ship leaking.'
> **Fourth paper.** – 'We commenced our voyage on Saturday, 30th Dec., 1865. Sunday, in the Channel, Monday, in open sea; Tuesday in ditto; Wednesday at Cowes; Thursday at Plymouth; Friday and Saturday at sea; Sunday bad weather; Monday water from the stern comes in cabins; the 9th, heavy damages, a boat lost. May we get home. Storm. – H. G.'
> **Fifth paper.** – 'F. C. McMILLAN, of Launceston, Tasmania, 11th of January, 1866, to his dear wife and dear children. May God bless you all. Farewell for this world. Lost in the steamship London, bound for Melbourne.'
> **Sixth paper.** – 'H. J. DENIS to Th. Denis Knight, at Great Shelford: Adieu father, brothers, and my … Edi … steamer, London, Bay of Biscay, Thursday, 10 o'clock. – Ship too heavily laden for its size, and too crank;

windows stove in; water coming in everywhere. God bless my poor orphans. Request to send this, if found, to Great Shelford. Storm not too violent for a ship in good condition.'

On the same day were found on the shoals of Quiberon, a binnacle watch stopped at half-past 10 o'clock, a woman's shift, two cotton sheets, two splinters of wood, having on them in white letters six centimetres (2½ inches) long the word 'London.' A great quantity of staves have been picked up along the coast.

(*The Times*, 1 Mar. 1866)

These messages must have distressed the family members who read them. It makes the realisation of a victim's last few moments all the more real and frightening – we can imagine someone desperately hunting for a scrap of paper, pencilling a few words on it, stuffing it into a bottle, sealing it, and then slinging it over the side. Each was a 'goodbye' that was not to be received until weeks after the writer's death, if at all. As Munro and others commented, many passengers wanted their families to know what had happened to them. Ships simply disappeared all too often in the nineteenth century and the long agonising wait for news, with the eventual realisation that there may never be any news at all, must have been almost unbearable. The victims wanted to spare their families this agony. The originals of these sad mementos were sent to relatives of the unfortunate writers.

It is remarkable that as many as six messages should even survive the stormy seas and be published. Survivors noted that a barrel containing many such notes had also been launched from the ship, but it was never found. However, there was one more voice still to speak from the depths of

Messages in bottles from the *London*'s victims were washed ashore.

the Bay of Biscay. Appropriately enough, the author was someone who had made a career from playing the dramatic final scene:

> TO THE EDITOR OF THE TIMES
> Sir – on Friday night I received the last written words of my dear husband. They were found in a bottle on the Brighton beach, and forwarded to me by Mr C. A. Elliott, of Trinity College, Cambridge. They are written in pencil on a torn envelope, and read as follows: –
> '11th of January, on board the London. We are just going down. No chance of safety. Please give this to Avonia Jones, Surrey Theatre. – GUSTAVUS VAUGHAN BROOKE.'
> Will you be kind enough to insert this fact in your valuable journal, for, sad as the message is, he has many friends who will be glad once more to hear from him, even though his words have come from his very grave. With respect, I remain sincerely yours,
> AVONIA BROOKE
> (*The Times*, 20 Mar. 1866)

Only one body was ever described in the newspapers. The corpse of Mrs Emily Debenham was washed ashore on the island of Hoëdic, Brittany, about a month after the disaster, and identified because she had sewn her name into her undergarments. Her identity was confirmed by her brother-in-law, Henry Debenham, on account of the distinctive rings that she wore. Henry brought the remains home for interment – the only SS *London* victim to be granted a family burial.

Ballads, Sermons and Poetry

Newspapers were not the only means by which important national news was conveyed to the population in Victorian England. A number of popular ballads were composed to mark the SS *London* disaster. Ballads utilised the long-standing oral tradition of conveying news to mark significant events and ensure they were not quickly forgotten. The words were often professionally printed as ballad sheets to sell to singers, although a lyricist is usually not identified. The Bodleian Library at Oxford University has a collection of ballad sheets that would have been sung in communities all around the UK. Their holding includes two examples related to the SS *London*. The first is entitled *Loss of the London* (Roud no. V6049), and is reproduced below:

> The sea ran high, the winds were wild,
> As thro' the waves the London toiled,
> Each lip was blanched, and terror there,
> Filled e'en the bravest heart with care;
> But on she passed through storm and rain,
> And tried to conquer, but in vain;
> For with two hundred souls or more,
> The London sank near a foreign shore.

> The scene was harrowing, children pressed,
> Against each loving mother's breast,
> And musing asked the reason why
> The tears stood in each parent's eye.
> The Captain said all hope was gone,
> And each one prayed 'Thy will be done,'
> And with two hundred souls or more
> The London sank near a foreign shore.
>
> One man was there who played his part,
> As one who had a Lion's heart;
> Brooke was the heroic actor's name,
> And history shall record his fame;
> He worked until all hope was gone,
> Then calmly paced the deck alone,
> And with two hundred souls or more
> The London sank near a foreign shore.

The second example in the Bodleian collection (Roud no. V15644) is much longer and was published by T. Pearson of Manchester.

The celebrated 'singing fisherman', Sam Larner, was a folksinger from Winterton in Norfolk who was recorded by the BBC in the 1950s. Born in 1878, he could still remember many ballads from earlier eras, having been taught them by his father. One of these concerns the *London* tragedy, and concludes with:

> In the Bay of Biscay, the sea ran high –
> Danger and death were approaching nigh;
> For in such seas none could prevail,
> And none could tell what those souls did feel.
>
> Oh Captain Martin around did look;
> With a mighty crash our topgallant mast broke.
> We worked like Britons all through that night,
> To save our vessel on that dreadful might.
>
> Two hundred and thirty-nine dear souls afloat.
> In the midst of a gale some took a boat;
> Of all our ship, nineteen were saved,
> Two hundred and twenty found a watery grave.

At times of national loss, the Church had an important role in bringing communities together, helping people to express their grief, and supporting the bereaved. Churches in Melbourne were hung with black; Revd Draper's congregation came to his church in mourning attire; and many sermons were preached on the subject of the SS *London* during the weeks that followed the tragedy. Most notably, Revd James Ballantyne gave a religious

The Wesleyan church where Daniel Draper had been minister became a focus of grief in Melbourne. (Richard Wills)

address to the city on 18 March at Erskine Church, Melbourne, almost as soon as the news broke in Australia and this was followed three days later by Revd John Eggleston's sermon in memory of the Revd Daniel Draper. Four days after this, Revd Wollaston's sermon, preached at Trinity Church, east Melbourne, was entitled 'Death's Warning Voice'. These and other church services were packed and many sermons were printed and sold so that a wider population could take some solace from their ministers' words. In England, too, sermons were preached; for example, the Revd Frederick Jobson's sermon at City Road Chapel, London, was so well received that he published it. Like some of the initial newspaper coverage, the sermons, naturally enough, focus on the religious devotion of the *London*'s victims and the example that they set to the population at large – you must keep the faith, even when staring death in the face.

The impact of the loss of the SS *London* was such that many people wanted to express their emotion about such a traumatic event. As a result, a large number of poems were written in an attempt to capture the nation's feelings. They may have been well-intentioned, but to modern eyes they are painfully sentimental and often badly written. For some reason many Victorian gentlemen fancied themselves as budding poets.

The most famous of these poems is a series of verses by William Topaz McGonagall, a man who loved to write about tragedy, but who is often credited as the worst poet in British history. He was so bad that audiences laughed, booed, and threw things at him when he gave public recitals. His poem about the *London* is dire, and like all of his poetry it is often unintentionally amusing.

The Wreck of the Steamer 'London' While on her Way to Australia (McGonagall)

'Twas in the year of 1866, and on a very beautiful day,
That eighty-two passengers, with spirits light and gay,
Left Gravesend harbour, and sailed gaily away
On board the steamship 'London,'
Bound for the city of Melbourne,
Which unfortunately was her last run,
Because she was wrecked on the stormy main,
Which has caused many a heart to throb with pain,
Because they will ne'er look upon their lost ones again.

'Twas on the 11th of January they anchored at the Nore;
The weather was charming — the like was seldom seen before,
Especially the next morning as they came in sight
Of the charming and beautiful Isle of Wight,
But the wind it blew a terrific gale towards night,
Which caused the passengers' hearts to shake with fright,
And caused many of them to sigh and mourn,
And whisper to themselves, We will ne'er see Melbourne.

Among the passengers was Gustavus V. Brooke,
Who was to be seen walking on the poop,
Also clergymen, and bankers, and magistrates also,
All chatting merrily together in the cabin below;
And also wealthy families returning to their dear native land,
And accomplished young ladies, most lovely and grand,
All in the beauty and bloom of their pride,
And some with their husbands sitting close by their side.

'Twas all on a sudden the storm did arise,
Which took the captain and passengers all by surprise,
Because they had just sat down to their tea,
When the ship began to roll with the heaving of the sea,
And shipped a deal of water, which came down on their heads,
Which wet their clothes and also their beds;
And caused a fearful scene of consternation,
And among the ladies great tribulation,
And made them cry out, Lord, save us from being drowned,
And for a few minutes the silence was profound.

Then the passengers began to run to and fro,
With buckets to bail out the water between decks below,
And Gustavus Brooke quickly leapt from his bed
In his Garibaldi jacket and drawers, without fear or dread,

And rushed to the pump, and wrought with might and main;
But alas! all their struggling was in vain,
For the water fast did on them gain;
But he enacted a tragic part until the last,
And sank exhausted when all succour was past;
While the big billows did lash her o'er,
And the Storm-fiend did laugh and roar.

Oh, Heaven! it must have really been
A most harrowing and pitiful scene
To hear mothers and their children loudly screaming,
And to see the tears adown their pale faces streaming,
And to see a clergyman engaged in prayer,
Imploring God their lives to spare,
While the cries of the women and children did rend the air.

Then the captain cried, Lower down the small boats,
And see if either of them sinks or floats;
Then the small boats were launched on the stormy wave,
And each one tried hard his life to save
From a merciless watery grave.

A beautiful young lady did madly cry and rave,
'Five hundred sovereigns, my life to save!'
But she was by the sailors plainly told
For to keep her filthy gold,
Because they were afraid to overload the boat,
Therefore she might either sink or float,
Then she cast her eyes to Heaven, and cried, Lord, save me,
Then went down with the ship to the bottom of the sea,
Along with Gustavus Brooke, who was wont to fill our hearts with glee
While performing Shakespearian tragedy.

And out of eighty-two passengers only twenty were saved,
And that twenty survivors most heroically behaved.
For three stormy days and stormy nights they were tossed to and fro
On the raging billows, with their hearts full of woe,
Alas! poor souls, not knowing where to go,
Until at last they all agreed to steer for the south,
And they chanced to meet an Italian barque bound for Falmouth,
And they were all rescued from a watery grave,
And they thanked God and Captain Cavassa, who did their lives save.

Having denigrated the hapless McGonagall, it is only fair to repeat that none of the other British poems published about the disaster at the time were great works of literature either. Here, for instance, is the verse written by poet Sidney Thompson Dobell to honour the memory of Captain Martin:

John Bohun Martin (Dobell)

> Keeping his word, the promised Roman kept
> Enough of worded breath to live till now.
> Our Regulus was free of plighted vow
> Or tacit debt: skies fell, seas leapt, storms swept;
> Death yawned: with a mere step he might have stept
> To life. But the House-master would know how
> To do the master's honours; and did know,
> And did them to the hour of rest, and slept
> The last of all his house. Oh, thou heart's-core
> Of Truth, how will the nations sentence thee?
> Hark! as loud Europe cries 'Could man do more?'
> Great England lifts her head from her distress,
> And answers 'But could Englishman do less?'
> Ah England! goddess of the years to be!

Some of the poems ran to enormous lengths. John Abraham Heraud's 'lyrical ballad' entitled *The Wreck of the London*, for example, was published as a book and ran to some forty-eight fairly painful verses. It is far too long to reproduce here, but a single verse may suffice to demonstrate the calibre and melodrama of the work:

> His trident the Sea-god raised; while he
> Weird words was heard to utter:-
> And set the Starboard Life-boat free,
> And stove in the Starboard Cutter.
> Then heavily rolled the Ship afeard,
> And dead astern the wind careered.

Although forty-eight verses seems extreme, it was not the longest piece of published poetry on the subject. This honour belongs to the Revd Samuel Ferguson, minister of Fortingall, Perthshire, who also considered himself a poet. Ferguson had travelled on the SS *London* himself in 1865; he had met Captain Martin and conducted public worship aboard ship on Sundays. In consequence, he created a fifty-seven verse *Elegy on the Loss of the Steamship London*, which includes 'copious historical notes' on the incident; and, as if fifty-seven verses were not enough, it is accompanied by an additional four-verse coda entitled *Epitaph for Those Who Perished in the Foundering of the 'London'*.

Apart from established British poets such as McGonagall, Dobell, and Heraud, the Australian poet Adam Lindsay Gordon also penned words in memory of the shipwreck. His poem *Lex Talionis* is far more accomplished than the shaky contributions from the UK, and includes this verse:

Adam Lindsay Gordon.
(State Library of Victoria)

> Ah! friend, did you think when the *London* sank,
> Timber by timber, plank by plank,
> In a cauldron of boiling surf,
> How alone at least, with never a flinch,
> In a rally contested inch by inch,
> You could fall on the trampled turf?
> When a livid wall of the sea leaps high,
> In the lurid light of a leaden sky,
> And bursts on the quarter railing;
> While the howling storm-gust seems to vie
> With the crash of splintered beams that fly,
> Yet fails too oft to smother the cry
> Of women and children wailing?

Members of the public in England and Australia also felt moved to try and express themselves in verse, and submitted their efforts to newspapers, where many were published. Often they are rather cumbersome efforts with oppressive sentimentality and heavy religious overtones but, throughout all these works, it is clear that it was not simply the shock of the heavy death toll that made the SS *London* newsworthy. The impact persisted in the months and years to come because the strong Christian faith of the passengers was seen as a good and proper lesson to everyone, especially since the moral conduct of persons at sea had often been the subject of such scepticism. However, once the public inquiry began and people started to ask more questions about the events on board the ship, a sense of controversy, even injustice, was equally important in perpetuating the memory of the disaster.

Books and Memorabilia

These days it would be considered highly offensive to sell some commemorative china or a set of postcards immediately after a motorway pile-up or terrorist atrocity but, in Victorian times, it was not uncommon to memorialise a tragedy in this way. Success and endeavour were celebrated, but death and disaster also had to be publicised and honoured appropriately; people perhaps wanted to feel connected to important events.

A popular range of Sunderland lustreware was produced soon after the loss of the *London* by potteries such as Moore & Company, based in Southwick on the River Wear. These all bear a transfer print of the ship, hand painted, and the phrase 'The Unfortunate London'; many are accompanied by a verse of emotional poetry. The most frequently encountered item is a large orange-and-white mug with an anchor and two patriotic mariners carrying Union Jack flags on the reverse, but a common variant omits the mariners on the back and carries instead the following lines, entitled 'Love':

> There's sunshine on the sea my love
> There's beauty o'er the skies,
> But fairer seem thy looks my love
> And brighter are thine eyes.

This verse seems to capture the longing that bereaved people have in trying to recapture the loving face of someone they have lost. Besides the

Lustreware mug produced in 1866 to memorialise the loss of the 'Unfortunate *London*'.

The foundering of the S.S. LONDON in the Bay of Biscay, Jan 11 1866.

Carte de visite, published to commemorate the loss of the SS *London*.

commemorative mugs, there were also plates and jugs in bright pink and orange, all depicting the *Unfortunate London*.

In addition to this, a range of pictures were released for sale by various enterprising photographers. These were small images of the kind known as *carte de visites*, which measure about 2.5 inches by 4 inches. Various images were produced. There were photographs of the survivors – particular the three passengers, Munro, Wilson and Main – but images of John King were also sold. In fact, since he came to be regarded as the main hero of events, at least one photographer in Melbourne actually advertised in the press that they had images of him for sale, while people sought out his autograph. Photographic images of Captain Martin and John King were converted into sketches by skilled artists and used to illustrate articles in newspapers and periodicals. Another popular *carte de visite* depicted an artist's impression of the last few minutes of the *London* as it began to go down, with King, Munro and colleagues looking on from the ship's cutter.

A series of books was also quickly published; the first on the scene, and the most popular, was entitled *The Wreck of the 'London'*, which appeared just a few weeks after the loss was reported. Its author, Gerard Moultrie, was an Anglican minister. Impressed by the exemplary Christian faith apparently displayed by the *London*'s victims, Moultrie speedily interviewed a number of the survivors as well as relatives of the deceased, and arranged for his book to be published. It sold well and, after the public inquiry was completed, he updated it and published a second edition. The book plucks at the heartstrings of a Victorian audience that enjoyed reading about death and heroism in a somewhat romanticised and sanitised fashion. The clear message throughout the text of the triumph of faith and courage

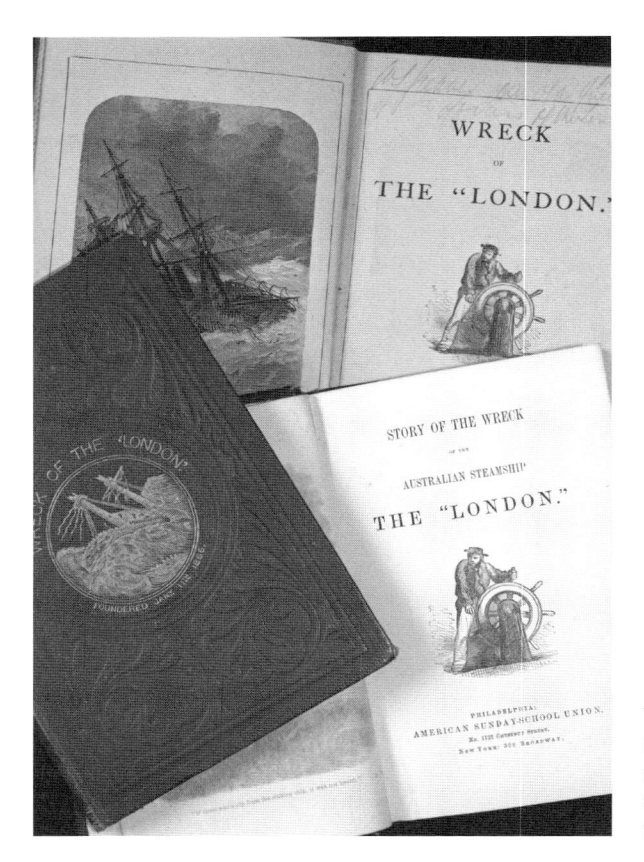

Various editions of Gerard Moultrie's books about the *London*, speedily published after the disaster.

over death meant that his work was even picked up by the American Sunday School Union and republished there as *Story of the Wreck of the Australian Steamship the 'London'*.

Other books followed, especially in Australia, with titles such as *The Loss of the 'London' on Her Passage from London to Melbourne* and *Sorrow on the Sea* both published in Melbourne. In Dunedin, New Zealand, John Munro published his own account of what happened, which was more critical of the *London*'s officers for doing so little to save the ship or its passengers. James Wilson gave a lengthy and detailed interview to the *Cornhill Magazine* that is more frank than many others, and includes details not found elsewhere.

The reaction to the loss of the SS *London* washed over the country like a huge melancholy wave, encompassing incredulity, personal grief, lessons in faith, national sorrow, a charitable fund, memorabilia, poetry, sermons, criticisms, and messages in bottles. In the midst of all this came the official inquiry. The Board of Trade was responsible for commercial shipping in 1866 and it had the legal obligation to investigate shipwrecks in which people died. It was a very public tragedy, and the inquiry was also to be a very public event.

STARTLING NARRATIVE!
AND
APPALLING CATASTROPHE!

WRECK
OF THE
STEAMSHIP, "LONDON,"
220
COLONISTS & EMIGRANTS LOST!
WITHIN THREE DAYS' SAIL OF PLYMOUTH.

19
SOULS ARE ALL THAT ESCAPED!

The Survivors were driven before the Gale, in the Cutter, for Twenty Hours before they were picked up, and had one very narrow escape of being swamped, the Boat being half filled with water.

Heroic Conduct of the eminent Tragedian, **G. V. BROOKE.**

THE CHIEF ENGINEER'S ACCOUNT.
LETTERS FROM THE MIDSHIPMAN, AND A FRIEND OF CAPTAIN MARTIN.
MEMOIRS OF DR. WOOLLEY AND REV. DANIEL J. DRAPER,
LIFE OF G. V. BROOKE.
And other Interesting Particulars of this ill-fated Vessel and its Crew, collected FROM AUTHENTIC SOURCES.

PROPOSED MEETING IN AID OF THE SURVIVORS.
ONE PENNY.

LONDON:—H. PEARCE, 32, LOWER KENNINGTON LANE; H. WILSON, 63, BERMONDSEY STREET; & ALL NEWS AGENTS.

Pamphlet comprising a 'startling narrative' of the wreck of the *London*, on sale for one penny in 1866. (Houghton Library, Harvard University. ref: Geog 4677.82)

10

The Inquiry

The Committee of the Privy Council for Trade were quick to order an official inquiry into the loss of the SS *London*. The Board of Trade was the government body responsible for all civilian maritime matters, and it had a duty to investigate matters of safety including the loss of British ships.

James Traill, stipendiary police magistrate, was appointed to head the investigation, accompanied by two nautical experts or 'assessors' to advise the inquiry board: Captain Henry Harris and Captain R. Baker. A solicitor named James O'Dowd conducted day-to-day proceedings on behalf of the Board of Trade, and led the process of gathering evidence from individual witnesses. Other legal representatives were also present. William Talfourd Salter appeared for the relatives of Mr and Mrs Thomas and their children, who had all died in the wreck. Alexander Burrell was a solicitor from Glasgow who attended the inquiry – it was he who unwittingly sent his young son to Melbourne on board the *London* in his stead. He represented himself as well as Mrs Tennant of Edinburgh, who had lost her husband. William Hitchcock represented the father of Mary Cutting, a passenger who perished. The venue was to be the police court at Greenwich in London, and proceedings were due to start on Monday 29 January 1866. The stage was set.

However, even before the inquiry officially began, it got itself into difficulties. As soon as Traill, the magistrate, realised that solicitors would be present representing the victims of the disaster he forbade them from asking any questions at the proceedings or cross-examining the witnesses. Sensing injustice, the press howled its derision. The Board of Trade would be seeking answers to questions about the safety of the SS *London* and the competence of its captain – both matters for which the Board itself had some responsibility – but only persons appointed by the Board of Trade would be allowed to ask questions. James Traill was a veteran of wreck investigations and hid behind the fact that it was customary not to allow cross-examination, which was true, and that the law (Merchant Shipping Act, 1854) did not sanction it. But it did not bar it either. The inquiry was an investigation; it was not a formal court of law – there would be no jury, no verdict, no sentencing – so it was at the discretion of the presiding magistrate to elect how the inquiry should gather its evidence, so long as the minimum stipulations of the Act were met.

Traill was so sensitive on this subject, which provoked much criticism, that he devoted a whole page to defending his decision in the opening to his official report. Tellingly, after quoting what the Merchant Shipping Act said on the subject, he went on to say:

> If this [the provisions of the Act] is not deemed a sufficient answer, we may notice the utter impossibility of carrying on an inquiry in which so many persons would be entitled to take part – the relations and friends of all the sufferers, the owners or underwriters of goods, the owners of the ship, and other persons interested, for all would be equally entitled, and many, no doubt, would claim to have the same privilege.

A victim's father later wrote that truth should have been more important than the inconvenience of Mr Traill organising a more searching inquiry, but Traill had his blinkers on. He notes haughtily that the inquiry board were aware of all the questions that needed to be asked, and he summarises the purpose of the inquiry very clearly:

> The direct object of the inquiry in this case is the cause of the loss of the 'London'. Beyond this, however, there is an ulterior and important object, viz to bring under the notice of the Board of Trade any facts or suggestions that may present themselves to our notice in the course of the examination, and which may seem to be of service in preventing the occurrence of a similar disaster in future, and thus to afford additional protection to life and property at sea.

When the inquiry opened, the court was crammed full. On certain days Robert Wigram attended among the spectators, but sometimes Clifford Wigram came instead; other shipowners also watched proceedings. During the mere two-and-a-half weeks of the inquiry, forty witnesses would be called to provide first-hand accounts, advice, information, and other evidence. They included twelve survivors of the wreck: John Jones (chief engineer), John Greenhill (second engineer), William Hart (carpenter's mate), Daniel Smith (boatswain's mate), Walter Edwards (midshipman), William Daniels, John King, Richard Lewis, Benjamin Sheals (all able seaman), and James Wilson, John Munro and David Main (all passengers). The other witnesses called to give evidence were:

- George Gladstone and George Barber, shipwright surveyors to the Board of Trade.
- Robert Taplin and Robert Galloway, engineer surveyors to the Board of Trade.
- Thomas Wawn, surveyor to Lloyd's Register of Shipping.

- Samuel Smith, Thomas North, William Bundock and James Johnson, employed by Money Wigram & Sons as shipwright, boatbuilder, sailmaker and draughtsman respectively.
- Thomas Harding, Robert Maxwell and Edward Humphreys, employed by Humphreys and Tennant who supplied the engines for SS *London*.
- Isaac Cole, ship's rigger and stevedore who helped prepare the SS *London* for sailing.
- James Lean, Peter Reeves, Samuel Cornish, John Forster, and John Stoll, all employed in connection with British emigration services.
- Alexander Gunn, clerk to the Registrar General of Seamen.
- Henry Caulier, employee of the Custom House in London.
- George Thompson, the Trinity House pilot that navigated SS *London* to Plymouth on its final voyage.
- William Bascombe, Admiralty overseer of ships built under contract for the Government.
- William Miller and Thomas Wilson, independent shipbuilders.
- Sir Daniel Cooper, a passenger on a previous voyage in the SS *London*.
- Robert Roe, a captain in the merchant service who knew Captain Martin.

Finally, James Traill permitted two relatives to briefly give evidence, maybe as a sop to the complaints that the families of the deceased had been denied input. Thomas Clough was the father of Robert Clough, a midshipman who died in the disaster, and Rion Benson was the brother of First Class passenger, Philip Benson.

It was all done very speedily: the inquiry began on 29 January 1866; the last witness was called on 14 February and the inquiry's conclusions were published on 5 March.

Professional Interactions and Expert Advice

The witnesses at the inquiry fell mainly into two camps: firstly experts who had examined the SS *London* or who had specialised knowledge relevant to the ship's demise, and secondly the survivors.

When professionals were called who had interacted with the ship or its crew, they came to defend their expert judgements. This was not surprising, because no-one wanted to be blamed for any kind of error that might have caused the disaster. Reading the inquiry report and newspaper coverage in the twenty-first century, it is notable that questions from the inquiry board were not very probing and that, by and large, an expert's opinion was taken at face value and not challenged or corroborated. It is conspicuous that none of Money Wigram's sons were called to give evidence; as the vessels' owners they had overall responsibility for the welfare of the ship, all the people on board, and its cargo.

George Gladstone, one of the Board of Trade's own surveyors, summarised the ship's construction and appearance, explaining that it met all regulations.

Having officially examined the ship on four occasions, he defended his inspections by proudly announcing that the SS *London* was 'as fine a ship as ever left the port of London'. Cold comfort, no doubt, to grieving relatives who read this quote in the newspapers. His colleague George Barber had the same role, but had not examined the ship personally. This left him more freedom to be critical because he did not have to defend his own reputation. His statement in the official report of the inquiry is considerably briefer than that of George Gladstone, but much more relevant. He stated clearly that similar ships to the *London* built on the Clyde would *not* have employed the same design – the poop would have been extended to cover the engine room hatch cover, providing it with much greater protection. He 'did not see why it might not have been carried out in the case of the *London*' and stated that, if the ship had been built on the Clyde, her engine room would have been protected in this way. This was the kind of direct criticism of the owners that Traill had wanted to avoid.

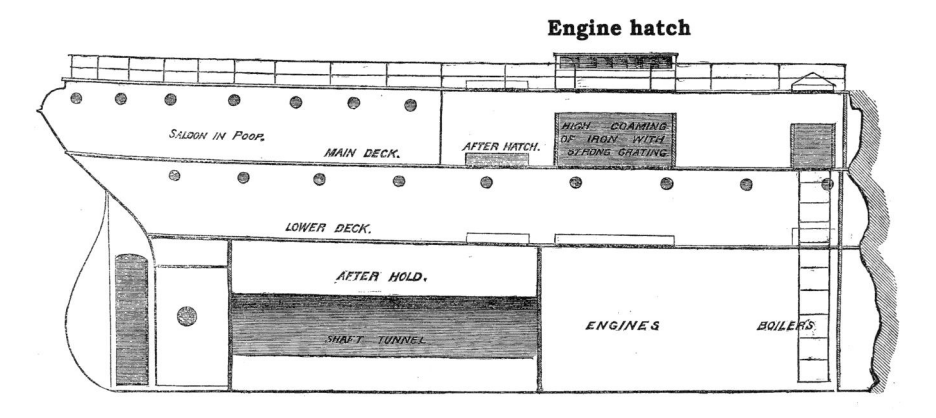

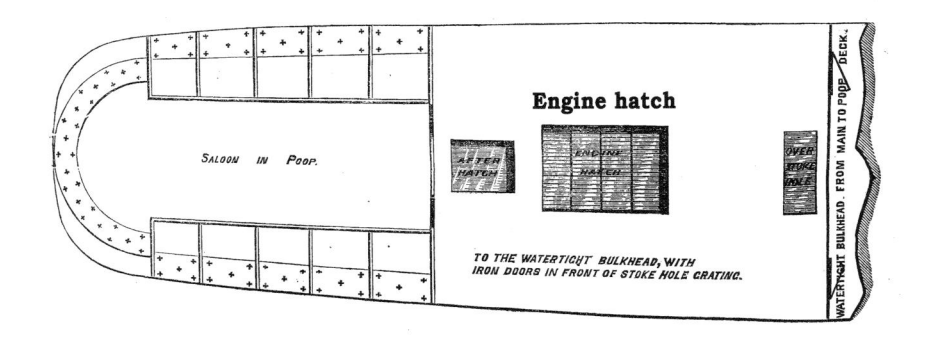

Sketches from George Barber, showing how the poop could be extended to cover and protect the engine hatch: longitudinal section through poop (top) and aerial view (bottom).

Barber also conceded that it was difficult to fix a maximum load line for any ship. A vessel could be too light as well as too heavily laden and it was a 'subject that required careful consideration'. This was a way of saying that there was no infallible method for ensuring that ships were not overloaded, and that the Board of Trade's own surveyor could not give concrete guidance.

Thomas Wawn, surveyor to *Lloyd's Register of Shipping* had, like Gladstone, inspected the ship for official purposes and he, of course, defended his assessment: 'I never saw a vessel better fitted than the *London*'. In particular, he felt that the original design of engine room hatch cover, if properly secured, ought to have been sufficient and that George Barber's suggested alternative design might not be appropriate.

Emigration officers were supposed to examine ships leaving British ports to ensure that they came up to the required standards for safety and seaworthiness. The officer at London who had signed off the SS *London* was James Lean, and he endorsed his own report. When asked about the number of boats a ship ought to carry, he was categorical: 'I do not consider it necessary that a ship should have boats sufficient to carry all the passengers from a ship'. He went on to explain that a ship could scarcely have space to accommodate enough boats for everyone, as if this was a rather self-evident remark.

Questioning from the panel revealed that Lean had not inspected the *London*'s sails because 'We don't think it likely that the Messrs Wigram, or any other respectable house, would deceive us'. He went on to reveal that not only had he *not* inspected them, but that he only received a list of them from the owners the day before he was due to testify. This embarrassing admission provoked laughter from the spectators. The *London* carried about eighty sails on board, but only two of these were 'storm sails' – made from the strongest canvas, which was less likely to split. The various emigration officers generally did not inspire confidence. The activities of the lax-sounding emigration official at Plymouth, Captain Stoll, have already been discussed in an earlier chapter, but at the inquiry he made it very clear that he did exactly what was expected of him – no less and certainly no more. It is difficult to avoid the impression that an emigration officer's role could be simply a 'tick-the-box' exercise, rather than the guardian of public safety that it was supposed to be.

The experts had their disagreements. Thomas Wawn, the surveyor from Lloyd's, claimed that nailing tarpaulin over a hatch cover should normally be sufficient to keep the water out, whereas William Bascombe from the Admiralty suggested that an iron grating ought to be used as on Royal Navy ships. Wawn admitted that he had been so satisfied with his official inspection of the SS *London* that he had applied to the Wigrams for his own son to join the ship as third engineer, but the position was already filled. This was a lucky escape for Wawn junior, although the ship's third engineer on its last voyage, John Armour, had been one of the survivors.

Little was reliably determined about whether the *London* was overloaded, because the national standards were so loose. The deep load line was the lowest depth that a ship ought to sit in the water when fully laden, but it was not marked on the side of the ship. It was calculated according to a formula that did not fully take account of the design of the ship and, when assessing safety, the calculated load line did not allow for how differently a heavily loaded ship might behave in stormy seas. The depth of loading for the *London* was determined by Money Wigram & Sons themselves and set at a draught of 20 feet and 3 inches. The draught is the distance from the surface of the water to the lowest part of the hull below water.

According to the customs official that testified, the ship was carrying a similar tonnage of cargo on her final voyage to Melbourne (1,308 tons) compared to her second outward voyage (1,347 tons). Isaac Cole who helped load the ship at East India Docks, recorded the ship's draught when fully laden in dock. He stated the draught was 20 feet at the bows and 20 feet, 9 inches at the stern. George Thompson, the pilot, measured the draught at Gravesend and found it to be 19 feet, 9 inches, and 20 feet, 9 inches respectively. He had taken similar measurements for her first and second voyages – on the second voyage it was 18 feet, 3 inches forward and 21 feet, 9 inches aft. Thompson recalled that Robert Harris, the chief officer, told him that he had nearly 9 feet of the vessel's side clear of the water and so had a foot to spare. Wawn, the Lloyd's Register agent, stated that any draught up to 21 feet and 3 inches would have been passed by him. Captain Stoll at Plymouth took no measurements but said he thought it looked all right, yet admitted it was difficult to see.

Some witnesses suggested the London was overladen. Thomas Wilson, an experienced shipbuilder, said he thought the load line had been set about 18 inches too high by Wigrams and should have been set at 18 feet and 9 inches, and that when laden to over 20 feet the ship would not rise to the sea but plough into it. Rion Benson, who lost a brother on the ship, commented that the ship sat so low in the water at Plymouth that the gangplank was level with the quayside.

During proceedings, Talfourd Salter and the other solicitors representing victims' families were ostensibly allowed to submit questions to Traill, who said he would endeavour to ask them. However, after four days of non-interaction with the various witnesses, Talfourd Salter could stand it no more. He stood up at the inquiry and declared that cross-examination was required to throw the fullest light on the events under investigation, and that, although he was quite aware that the magistrate was pursuing the usual practice for inquiries of this type, 'it might not be the course best calculated to elicit the truth'. Traill countered that cross-examination 'would lead to great inconvenience' and hoped that his legal colleague would stay to observe proceedings. Talfourd Salter, however, regretting the embarrassment it would cause to the inquiry, insisted that it was his duty to leave, and he promptly walked out. This was about as rude as one lawyer might be to another in public: Talfourd Salter was asserting that the proceedings were so inadequate that he did not wish to be professionally associated with them. This was the most awkward moment of the inquiry for Traill.

The Survivors' Tales

In many ways, of course, the witnesses that attracted the greatest attention in terms of media coverage were the survivors. Between them, their recollections provided an account of what happened on board the *London* in its last few days. There were some inconsistencies between the various accounts, as the witnesses had different roles on board the ship, they were in different places at crucial times, and because the human brain is imperfect when recalling past events. Where they differed was in the detail, and this occasionally frustrated the inquiry board. For example, Smith and Hart asserted that attempts were made to lift up the damaged engine-hatch cover and move it back to position, but that ultimately their attempts to do so were thwarted by it being smashed to pieces. Conversely, midshipman Edwards insisted that he saw no attempts made to reapply the cover and that it lay intact on deck throughout the *London*'s final day.

One of the most crucial pieces of new evidence was first brought up by survivor William Hart, the carpenter's mate. The flying jib boom had been torn away from the ship by the storm and for some time could not be retrieved. When, eventually, it was brought back on board, he testified that it was laid alongside the engine-room hatchway, where it was lashed down. It was a large and heavy piece of mast timber up to 1 foot thick, and was laid flat on the deck underneath the projecting edge of the hatch cover. He suggested that, when the heavy sea assaulted the ship, the boom could have acted like a lever in concert with the destructive power of the sea to prise

Five of the survivors who testified at the inquiry: from left to right Main, Munro, Gardner, King and Wilson. (National Library of Australia. Uncatalogued item; incorrectly dated to 1854; Munro and King are misidentified in the original)

off the hatch cover. Other survivors also noticed the flying jib-boom in the vicinity of the hatch cover, but there was some disagreement about how securely it was tied down, if at all.

There were moments of poignancy during the survivors' testimonies. Engineer John Greenhill broke down and sobbed on recalling his last conversation with Captain Martin, and there must have been silence when Walter Edwards talked about passengers' reactions to knowing that they were all going to die. There were surprising revelations too. Passenger John Munro complained to the inquiry board that the crew had been curiously unhelpful in baling out water and operating the ship's pumps, and that this work had been undertaken almost exclusively by passengers themselves. When he went to remonstrate with the boatswain, he found him compiling a list of seaman who were too ill to work, despite the ship being in a sinking condition – there were twenty-one names on his list. Both Munro and another passenger, David Main, complained that the hatches were not watertight and admitted lots of water.

In an age where temperance was much prized, there was praise from the inquiry board for young midshipman Edwards for hiding one bottle of ship's brandy from the survivors who had escaped the *London*. Yet, ironically, one survivor turned up at the inquiry drunk. To the consternation of the press, the board, and everyone else present, it became clear during his increasingly incoherent testimony that able seaman Richard Lewis was somewhat inebriated. Lewis's testimony was interrupted and he was ordered out – another awkward moment.

It must have been an intimidating experience for the survivors – who were mainly working-class men – to be hauled up in front an official inquiry board and made to give evidence in public. Perhaps Richard Lewis resorted to alcohol for Dutch courage. Nonetheless, the survivors' accounts established the basic facts about the SS *London*'s last days and the sequence of events, even if the exact timings and details varied between witnesses. Where survivors differed in their recollections, it is only fair to state that limited effort was made by the inquiry board to try and reconcile or challenge these differences.

Nonetheless the accounts given by survivors did establish that Captain Martin managed to keep the SS *London* sailing 'head to the wind' during its final days. This means that the vessel's bows were kept facing towards the direction from which the wind was blowing. It was an important point because a ship that was put before the wind – i.e., the wind was blowing at it from behind – was at greater risk of damage during a storm. Many commentators assumed that Captain Martin *had* put the *London* before the wind, and that this action had contributed to the ship's loss. On this issue, therefore, the captain was deemed not to be at fault.

Yet another one of those 'awkward moments' occurred towards the end of the inquiry when a man called John Clare leapt up and suddenly asked to address the inquiry. He was a shipbuilder in the middle of a long-running dispute with the Admiralty because his patented method for constructing iron ships had been adopted by the Royal Navy without compensation.

He had been 'allured', he said, by some letters in newspapers to come forward and make a statement. The Board of Trade solicitor, O'Dowd, spoke to him briefly but felt he had nothing useful to offer. John Clare ignored him and still attempted to address the inquiry but Traill, no doubt aware of the political sensitivities around his relationship with the Admiralty, would not allow him to speak and forced him to stop.

Rather bizarrely, the inquiry called a random previous passenger from an earlier voyage of the *London* to give evidence. There is no indication as to how or why Sir Daniel Cooper was selected, but he had no professional maritime role or seafaring experience. He had sailed on the *London*'s maiden voyage to Melbourne in 1864 and said that the ship was sluggish, did not rise to the sea, performed poorly under sail, and had the appearance to the eye of being deeply laden. He said: 'I did not like her behaviour and although I had every confidence in Captain Martin, I would never have gone to sea in her again'. Sir Daniel's disapproving testament was met with silence; no questions were asked.

A similarly strange choice of witness was county magistrate Robert Roe, who had known Captain Martin when they were both junior officers on sailing ships. He testified to Martin being a 'very proper man to take charge of a ship'. It must have seemed peculiar to everyone present that the only witness produced to testify to Captain Martin's character and professional ability was not his current employer, but someone who had worked with him twenty years ago. Roe was asked no questions, but what useful questions could anyone ask? After this concluding, rather odd, testament the inquiry closed.

This, then, very briefly was the official inquiry. A curiously staged and unsatisfying affair that did not really get to the heart of anything much, except to recognise that the loss of the engine-hatch cover was the fundamental problem that caused the SS *London* to be lost. The bereaved families, media, shipping industry, and public alike awaited the inquiry's report, hoping for some clear-cut analysis of how this tragedy had occurred.

The Inquiry's Findings

The report ran to over sixty pages when complete with its foreword – an unprecedented length for a wreck inquiry – but it took less than three weeks to reach its conclusions. The final version was formally published by order of the House of Commons so that the public could buy a copy.

The inquiry concluded that the SS *London* was in all respects a good vessel as far as its seaworthiness was concerned. It noted that the majority of professional witnesses thought the vessel was not overladen, and that the cargo appeared to have been stored correctly.

The weather when the *London* left Plymouth at just after midnight on the morning of 6 January was calm and heralded no storm. Local measurements presented by officials at Plymouth, including Captain Stoll, did not indicate a falling barometer and so an imminent deterioration in the weather had not been anticipated. This was an exoneration for Captain Martin – he had not rashly headed out to sea when bad weather was inevitable in order to

MINUTES OF EVIDENCE.

INQUIRY into the Circumstances attending the Loss of the Screw Steam Ship "London," on the 11th of January 1866, in the *Bay of Biscay*, made by direction of the Board of Trade, by *James Traill*, Esq., Stipendiary Magistrate, assisted by Captains *Harris* and *Baker*, acting as Assessors.

Greenwich Police Court, 29th January 1866.   29 January 1866.

GEORGE JOSEPH GLADSTONE, Sworn:

I RESIDE at Blackwall. I am Shipwright Surveyor to the Board of Trade, and Senior Surveyor for the Port of London. It is part of my duty to survey passenger steam-ships occasionally during their construction. I go, from time to time, at no stated periods. I saw the ship "London" while she was building; I first saw her while she was in frame. She was the property of the Messrs. Wigram & Sons. This book contains the official entries respecting the ship, made by myself. I went, I should say, four different times to the yard during the building up to her launching. I saw her before she was in frame, when in frame, when the deck was laid, and before she was launched. According to my judgment the materials with which she was constructed were of the first quality: the materials were angle-iron frame, iron beams, stringer plates and kelsons; the plating of the bottom was of iron; the kelsons were plate kelsons. The garboard streak plates were 7–8ths of an inch thick; the streaks above the garboard streaks, for 13 streaks up, were 3–4ths of an inch thick, and from thence to the gunwale 11–16ths of an inch. She was double riveted from keel to gunwale; all her fastenings were sound and good, with stringer plates to all her decks, and beams properly fastened. She had four bulk-

Opening page of the inquiry report.

meet his sailing schedule. In fact the ship's master is roundly praised, based on his career record:

> Her master, Captain Martin, was a skilful and experienced seaman, and had commanded the ship from her first going afloat in 1864. His high professional character, and his great self-possession, manifested by his conduct in the trying circumstances in which he was placed, afford reasonable ground to believe that there was no defect of ability, vigilance, or energy on his part; and this ought to be borne in mind when, owing to the very defective state of the evidence as given by the survivors, there may be considerable difficulty in forming a judgment as to the cause or causes leading to the loss of his ship.

Notice that the disagreements between survivors' accounts are here magnified to protect the authority figure of Captain Martin who, being dead, could not testify. The inquiry concluded that, because the captain had behaved honourably in the ship's last hours and had never wrecked a ship before, he must in all other respects be a faultless professional. This was clearly a non sequitur.

Further relief for the memory of Captain Martin came when the inquiry found that he did not put his ship before the wind, so had not exposed the *London* to undue danger. Meanwhile the survivors' testimonies – mostly working-class men – are criticised as 'imperfect and confused'.

The report suggests that, although there is no conclusive evidence to confirm it, there is the possibility that the flying jib-boom stored on the main deck may have contributed to the unshipping of the engine-room hatch cover. It was also possible that the cover was either not fastened down properly, despite evidence from both engineers that it was, or that it was not sufficiently strongly constructed. Either way, the sea getting into the engine room by this route was undoubtedly the immediate cause of the ship's loss.

This being so, it was needless to discuss other matters such as the stowage of bags of coal on the ship's deck. Survivors agreed that coal was rolling around the deck and had blocked the scuppers that drained water off the main deck, but this was irrelevant.

Similarly, the inquiry picked up that merchant ships always seemed to go to sea fully masted – as did the *London* – with the topmost section of the masts (royal masts) in place with their associated spars. This risked wild weather ripping them away, as had in fact happened on board the *London*. Although not an immediate cause of the vessel's loss, it was to be deprecated: 'We think the practice a bad one, and hope that this inquiry may have the effect of inducing caution for the future'.

The report's summary eulogises Captain Martin a last time. If there were any other areas of criticism or potential fault that have been overlooked, it concludes, then readers should bear in mind that 'it is but reasonable to give the master credit for the character he always possessed, of being an

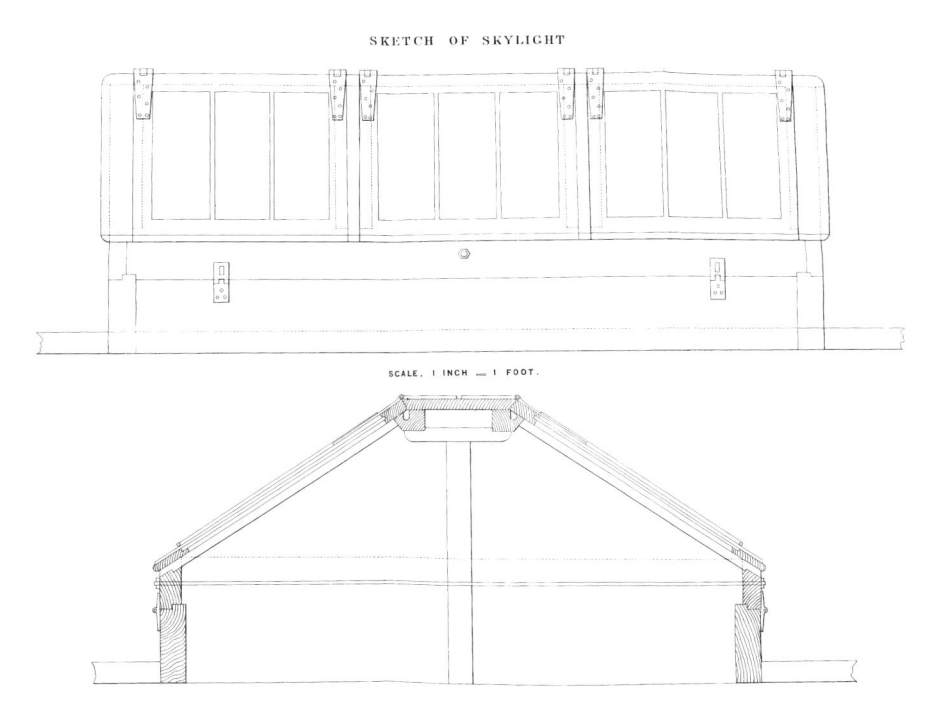

Diagram of the SS *London*'s engine-hatch cover – the glass-panelled roof (top) and shed-shaped cross-section.

able and careful seaman, who would not be guilty of any great default of management'.

However, for the future, shipwrights are implored to ensure that all hatchways are as strong as the decks of the ships to which they belong. Consideration ought to be given to using iron gratings to protect hatchways or to extending the poop of ships to cover them, as expert witnesses had suggested. Always, demands the report, steps should be taken to ensure that hatch covers are properly secured by the crew when at sea. The portholes at the stern of the ship ought also to be properly protected from damage as part of their design.

In its final paragraph, regarding the vital concern of the weight of a ship's cargo, the report did allow an implied criticism of the prevailing methods for establishing whether a vessel like the SS *London* was overladen or not:

> The rule of calculating the deep load line by the scale of displacement may be a safe one as regards the ship's ability to carry her cargo safely, but not as to her ability to carry her cargo lightly, so as to make her an easy ship for the conveyance of passengers. In calculating the deep load line, the question of buoyancy is a most material element as regards the behaviour of the ship in bad weather; and, in fact, were the deep load line permanently marked on all vessels, we might not have to deplore the annual loss of life that occurs from presumed over-loading. This is a subject which seems deserving of consideration.

Criticisms of the Inquiry

It is easy to criticise the inquiry itself. It was, however, fairly typical of the process employed at the time. There was clearly a haste to get it all over and done with quickly. Traill himself remarked that allowing more witnesses or a wider cross-examination would simply prolong matters but, as solicitor William Talfourd Salter pointed out, the traditional process was unlikely to get to the truth. Yet Traill had a blueprint for conducting the inquiry – he'd done others before – and he was determined to follow it. He and his advisers chose the witnesses to be called and they also decided upon the questions to ask. With the media, relatives, and shipowners scrutinising every word in the inquiry room, Traill was under pressure to get on with it.

Professional witnesses that had been involved with the *London* arrived simply to defend what they had done – be they emigration officer, designer, stevedore, or Lloyd's assessor. The lack of probing cross-examination meant there was little criticism of them, and these experts went largely unchallenged. It was, by and large, a gentle exercise, and of course there was that old question of why cross-examination had not been allowed. Or, rather, why James Traill had chosen not to allow it since it was at his discretion. That question kept coming back to bite him in the press.

Key questions were not asked and ideas for improved safety were left unexplored. There were potential regulatory issues here that impacted on future safety at sea and they were not addressed, so owners were left to continue to do as they pleased. These issues included:

1. Is it reasonable that shipowners should decide for themselves what the load line is on their ships? Does there need to be regulation or an evidence-based, independent assessment of how the line should be calculated? Does there need to be a wider safety margin for long-distance passenger ships carrying cargo compared to lightly crewed coastal cargo vessels?
2. If other commercial shipbuilders and the Royal Navy already knew about better ways to protect the engine-hatch cover – such as iron grids, higher surrounds, or extended poop decks – why did Money Wigram employ a different design when the ship was built? What justification did they have for using it?
3. The launching of the *London*'s lifeboats was poorly organised and many mistakes were made. Why was it that the iron pinnace sank? It was the ship's largest boat and, if it had been safely launched, then many more people might have been saved. Should these vital craft be made of iron? Why was the launching of the second pinnace delayed so much that it was too late? Why did the Board of Trade not recommend that crews practise the launching procedure? Was it time to review the regulations about the design of boats, their launching procedure, and the number of lifeboats carried? Why were three of them destroyed before they could even be launched?
4. Why was it so difficult to get an accurate list of everyone on board after the ship sank? The *London*'s records were ultimately Captain Martin's responsibility, but he was so lax that he even had to be reprimanded for it by UK port officials after the ship's maiden voyage. According to the inquiry, the *London* had space for 400 passengers. So, was it really only carrying a mere 170?
5. Who should decide what types of sail a ship should carry? The *London* lost vital sails ripped open by the wind, and this might not have happened if appropriate storm sails had been available.

Many of the inquiry's witnesses also failed to attract credibility. Taplin, one of the engineer surveyors to the Board of Trade, admitted he had never even been to sea. Lean, the emigration officer for London, confessed that he had little experience of steamships and that the *London* was the first ever steamship he had cleared from the port of London. Robert Roe was selected to give a character reference for Captain Martin, but he had not seen him for over twenty years. The testimony of Stoll, the emigration officer at Plymouth, shows he was clearly slack in his responsibilities. The shipbuilder Wilson had retired ten years before and so was hardly qualified to comment on modern vessels.

Many of the other witnesses were either employed by the SS *London*'s owners or beholden to them: Samuel Smith, Thomas North, William Bundock, and James Johnson were employed by Money Wigram & Sons directly; Thomas Harding, Robert Maxwell and Edward Humphreys worked for the engineers that Wigrams always used on its ships; Isaac Cole was paid by Wigrams to prepare the SS *London* for sailing; George Thompson was the pilot that Wigrams always used on the Thames. Thomas Wawn from Lloyd's Register worked for Money Wigram's brother, and was close enough to the family to try and beg a job for his son. Not unexpectedly, all of these witnesses offered no criticism of the SS *London* or its owners.

The reliability of the survivors as witnesses was also not commented upon, apart from able seaman Lewis, who was dismissed for turning up drunk to the inquiry. And yet the chief engineer of the *London*, John Jones, allegedly did not have the requisite first-class certificate to serve on the ship and had never served in any other vessel in a similar capacity. The midshipman Walter Edwards gave evidence that sometimes conflicted with statements from more practised seamen, but the SS *London* had been his first ever voyage: his entire career consisted of only a few days' seagoing experience.

It is particularly notable that none of the ship's owners were asked to give evidence at the inquiry. Robert, Clifford, and Charles Wigram were responsible for managing Money Wigram & Sons but were not called. In more recent times, the responsibility of owners has been clearly recognised and their involvement in any investigation after a disaster has been seen as integral – as, famously, to give just two examples, in the *Titanic* inquiry (1912) and that of the *Herald of Free Enterprise* (1987). However, in 1866, the Wigrams were not questioned. Yet they had appointed Captain Martin, authorised the designs of the SS *London*, appointed its safety features such as lifeboats, created the expectation that this was a fast ship, agreed its sailing schedule, and approved the quantity of cargo and its stowage. These were all matters relevant to the inquiry; Clifford Wigram had personally supervised the loading of the cargo but the witness called to testify about this matter was a lowly stevedore.

Victorian society generally deferred to persons of wealth, class and authority: they were assumed to be respectable, honourable and trustworthy, unless proven otherwise. This was the accepted order of things and it did not do to examine a gentleman's affairs too closely.

Yet perhaps the SS *London* disaster would be different because so many people from all walks of life had died. In these circumstances, would Victorian society tolerate an establishment inquiry that was so deficient? Would it be permitted to go unchallenged?

II
The Aftermath

The release of the inquiry report provoked considerable indignation because it was seen at best as inadequate and, at worst, as a cover up. The whole proceedings had been reported word for word in major national newspapers such as *The Times*, *Daily Telegraph*, and *The Standard*. Letters to the press from all around the British Empire expressed the frustration of writers that there had been a heavy loss of life, and yet no-one was being held responsible. Perhaps more than that – in an age where individuals did not generally sue for compensation in the wake of a disaster – was the realisation that nothing of significance had been learned, or would change, to prevent similar disasters in the future.

A letter survives from James Traill that he sent to Thomas Farrer, secretary of the Board of Trade, five days into the inquiry. The inquiry was such an important event that this communication would almost certainly have been seen by the Minister himself, Thomas Milner Gibson. The letter shows that Traill was frustrated, anxious, and unsure of his role, even after the inquiry had begun. Traill was irritated by the behaviour of Talfourd Salter, the solicitor of the bereaved relatives who had stormed out, and equally annoyed for having to take the public flak for denying any cross-examination. He was particularly concerned because he knew that an MP, Sir John Pakington, had raised the 'cross-examination question' in the House of Commons once already and was about to do so again. Traill's letter also reveals his unease that the inquiry was being placed in an awkward position – either acting as judge and jury against the owners, or producing a bland inconclusive 'summary of events' that would please no-one. Traill begs for guidance:

My dear Sir,

I see that Sir J Pakington is to repeat his question tomorrow, and I hope it will receive a conclusive answer. I have hitherto taken upon myself the odium (unreasonable as it is) of refusing to hear counsel. I could safely have warded this off by referring the counsel, Mr Talfourd Salter, to the Act of Parliament showing that I had no authority to hear any[one] but the person appointed by the Board of Trade to manage the case and that, if he wished to be heard, he should apply to the Board to be so appointed ...

The real difficulty, however, is to justify the inquiry itself ... The Board [of Trade] is putting into operation a very stringent inquiry, pointed directly against a person (the owner) who is not on his trial, nor his defence, but whose interest may be most seriously compromised by the proceedings, if unfavourable, and yet would not be protected by the result of the most favourable inquiry ...

If the Board [of Trade] expects that in the report we shall express an opinion as to the cause of loss, whether it was by a <u>fault</u> or with the <u>privity</u>* of the owner, or, short of that, that it arose from some <u>other cause</u> than <u>perils of the sea</u>, we shall, as I have said, be prejudicing the owner's defence in any actions brought against him.

I asked you in a former letter what is the practice in similar cases of reports. We may either state our opinion <u>explicitly</u>, or sum up the evidence leaving the Board [of Trade] to draw its own conclusions. If we do the former, I shall have to impose a very difficult and ungracious task upon the assessors, for the <u>finding</u> must be theirs, or if we adopt the latter course I fear our report will not satisfy the public, who will think our mountain has produced a very small mouse.

*Privity implied a legal responsibility for bringing about the loss of the ship as the result of failing to act upon some knowledge that the vessel was at risk.

The next day, Traill was given full reassurance in writing and urged by the Minister's office to 'give an opinion on the cause of loss if it is possible to form one' and that he was presiding over 'an inquest not a trial'. However, Traill was clearly unhappy about his inquiry delivering an opinion and he did not want to do it. This perhaps largely explains why the report's findings were somewhat bland. Incidentally, Traill also wrote to Farrer to seek confirmation of his stance on allowing cross-examination of witnesses and Farrer confirmed that it would be impractical and could not be allowed under the Act that governed the convening of the inquiry.

Separately, James O'Dowd, the solicitor appointed by the Board of Trade to organise the inquiry, wrote privately to the Minister, Thomas Milner Gibson. He assured the Minister that he 'did not in any way interfere with' the inquiry's decision to disallow cross-examination: 'I left the question as to the claim of counsel to cross-examine on behalf of the representatives of the lost passengers entirely in the hands of the court'. In other words, O'Dowd knew that cross-examination was permissible but that it would be awkward to allow it; hence, he did not assist.

This insight into the anxieties of the inquiry's magistrate and the secret machinations of a Victorian government department is valuable because of what was to come.

These behind-the-scenes debates were, of course, not made public at the time, but the press formed its own opinions about the inquiry's final report:

> The total loss of a first-rate passenger ship on the high seas is, happily, so rare an event that a certain degree of mystery still attaches to the fate of the London. The foundering of such a vessel, classed 'AA1' on Lloyd's List, but five days after the commencement of her voyage, in a gale which smaller craft rode out with safety, and in which one of her own boats was able to live, constitutes a leading case among nautical disasters, and justifies to some extent the feeling of dissatisfaction which has been so freely expressed. This feeling has not been allayed by the publication of the official Report to the Board of Trade, which imputes no blame to anyone.
> (*The Times*, 21 Mar. 1866)

One anonymous letter to the same newspaper even suggested that Wigrams had recognised that their ship was at risk and had taken particular steps to protect their own financial interest:

> A few days after the loss of the London I was given to understand by a gentleman connected with a large marine insurance-office that Messrs. Wigram had insured the London at his office for a large amount just previous to her departure, in addition to their own insurance fund.
>
> Now, if this should prove to be the case, the public have a right to know whether the extra weight of insurance was caused by any fear on the part of Messrs. Wigram of the extra weight of her cargo.
> (*The Times*, 23 Mar. 1866)

Debate in Parliament

As far as MP Sir John Pakington was concerned, he waited until the inquiry had delivered its conclusions before introducing a debate on the loss of the SS *London* in the House of Commons. His opening salvo on 19 March 1866 makes his opinions very clear:

> The sea-going public who have to travel between this kingdom and the colonies are specially exposed to two sources of danger. The one the desire of profit which prompts the shipowners to overload their vessels, the other the eagerness with which rival companies compete in conveying their passengers with the utmost possible speed.
> *(Hansard*, 19 Mar. 1866)

Then Sir John went further, and openly criticised the SS *London* inquiry and the process by which it had arrived at its conclusions:

> I stand here as one of the public, and as such I have no hesitation in saying that in my opinion that inquiry was a mockery and a delusion as far as it regarded the great question of the public safety ... We must, if we can,

Sir John Pakington.

guard the public for the future; and looking at the matter from that point of view, I say that that investigation was utterly futile for any purpose of discovering what were the real causes of the unfortunate calamity to which I am referring.

He severely criticised the inquiry for not allowing cross-examination of witnesses, and then went on to attack it for focusing on protecting the owners of the SS *London* from blame, rather than ascertaining causes and faults so that the public might be better protected in future. This was exactly what James Traill had feared, and he had written to the highest levels of the Board of Trade expressing these fears. The Minister himself must have been aware of that letter. Sir John was highly disapproving:

> It was imperatively necessary that that inquiry should be conducted with the most jealous regard to the public interests, and the public interests only; and that it should not assume the character – which I am sorry to say beyond all doubt it did assume – of an inquiry the object of which was to protect the owners of the vessel from blame.

While the Minister for the Board of Trade, Thomas Milner Gibson, sat there and squirmed beneath the onslaught, Sir John read out to the House two letters from relatives of passengers who had died on the London. Both were incensed that justice did not seem to have been done. A brother of James

Thomas, whose lawyer Talfourd Salter had walked out of the inquiry 'in disgust', wrote that:

> Nothing but one-sided testimony appeared to be sought. To those who watched the proceedings they appeared to be mainly an examination of officials by a tribunal of their own.

It also emerged that, although bereaved families and their legal representatives were supposedly permitted by James Traill to hand him written questions to be asked of the inquiry's witnesses, the magistrate frequently declined to ask the questions submitted to him. Sir John ticked off critical aspects of the disaster one by one that the inquiry had not properly addressed, while the Minister for the Board of Trade put on a brave face: the observation by many experienced men that the *London* was overladen, the coals stored on deck, the inadequate inspections by a series of emigration officers, the potentially bad design of the ship, the presence of so many seamen on board who could not speak English ... None of these points had been properly examined in the inquiry, maintained Sir John, and the government was to blame:

> Inquiries of this nature should be *bona fide*, if they are not so conducted as to elicit the truth there had better be no inquiries at all – they are mere delusions; you are deceiving the public, you are throwing dust in their eyes.

However, in closing, Sir John Pakington did admit that there was one small part of the report that he did agree with:

> There is one solitary passage in the report to which I am able to give my concurrence; it is where Mr. Traill, at the conclusion, says that it would be most desirable that the deep load-line should be marked on our passenger ships, and I hope my right honourable Friend will give serious consideration to that suggestion.

Sir John Pakington sat down and the Minister for the Board of Trade, Thomas Milner Gibson immediately stood up to reply. To James Traill's undoubted mortification, Milner Gibson began by publicly blaming the magistrate entirely for not allowing cross-examination of witnesses, even though the Minister's own secretary had reassured Traill that he should not permit it:

> The Act of Parliament is entirely silent as to whether counsel for any of the persons interested, directly or indirectly, have a right to be heard. My own opinion, and that of those I have consulted, is that that was a matter entirely within the discretion of the presiding magistrate of the court. All I can say is that if Mr. Traill, who was the presiding magistrate, had thought fit to allow the counsel on behalf of the relatives of passengers

who perished to cross-examine witnesses, Mr. O'Dowd would have made no objection.

Now we learn why O'Dowd was so keen to let the Minister know privately that he had not 'intervened' in this matter – it allowed Milner Gibson to blame this very unpopular decision on someone else. The Minister went on to distance himself as far as possible from the inquiry by telling the House that, although better witnesses might have been called to the inquiry, their selection had also been completely the responsibility of the inquiry board.

Milner Gibson's whole response was not about learning lessons, public safety, liability, or anything else except dodging personal responsibility for the inquiry. He conceded that the law about wreck inquiries perhaps needed some amendment but he did not commit himself to action. He avoided all reference to the culpability of the owners. Ludicrously, after admitting that the inquiry process was probably in need of attention, he then proceeded to defend its inadequate conclusions – damning the unfortunate James Traill with faint praise in the process:

> My honest opinion is that the inquiry into the loss of the *London* was a very searching inquiry, and I believe there was no failure of justice, although I admit there were some unpleasant circumstances connected with the inquiry. I believe that Mr. Traill endeavoured, to the best of his ability, to arrive at a just conclusion. While admitting that these inquiries

Thomas Milner Gibson.

as at present conducted may be improved, I must observe that they have [in the past] produced great benefits to the navigation of the country.

We were only anxious to have the most full and searching inquiry that was possible; our only desire was to arrive at the real cause of the wreck. I believe the report is not satisfactory as to the real cause of the wreck; and I imagine that it could not be otherwise than unsatisfactory, because the evidence leaves the real cause doubtful.

Cleverly, Milner Gibson then deflected the whole debate on to the adequacy of wreck inquiries in general, rather than the specific matter of the SS *London*. Having wriggled off the hook personally, the debate in the House thereafter centred almost entirely on the correct process for running wreck inquiries – probably to Milner Gibson's great satisfaction. Bizarrely, in the midst of this debate, one MP, Joseph Samuda, even stated that existing inquiries and inspection of ships were already *too* rigorous and burdensome for shipowners, who ought to be allowed to manage their own affairs. As an illustration of the 'unfairness' of the present system of inquiry, he noted:

> The Act of Parliament contemplated that if there was fault on the part of the owners the parties who suffered from the death of relatives should have redress to the extent of £15 a ton of measurement of the vessel. On this calculation the owners of the *London* would have been answerable, assuming the accident to have occurred through their default, to the extent of £25,000.

How terrible that a shipping company might actually have to pay compensation for deaths that it caused! It is a dramatic illustration of the reasons for senior figures being reluctant to criticise Money Wigram & Sons – £25,000 was a large sum in 1866, and this was not a society familiar with compensation claims of anywhere near this size. Where would it end, if honest leaders of British industry were held financially responsible for deaths of their employees or the public? Another MP even protested that Sir John Pakington had behaved very improperly by raising the issue in the House in the way that he had done; in doing so, he had dared to 'impugn the conduct' of the gentlemen who owned the SS *London*.

Ongoing debate was somewhat stifled by the rules of the House of Commons at the time, which stipulated that no MP could address the House twice in the course of the same debate, unless the House consented; so any further challenge from Sir John Pakington or any argument between him and Thomas Milner Gibson was out of the question. And so the 'debate' ground to a halt with no definite conclusions, and the House moved on to the much more important matter of financing the Royal Navy in India.

The Campaigning Lawyer

Meanwhile, another figure emerged to bring down criticism on the inquiry and the SS *London*'s owners. That person was lawyer Edward Gilbert Highton. His brother-in-law, Henry Dennis, had died on the *London* and had written one of the messages in bottles found after the ship went down. The text as reported in the newspapers had been incomplete and contained errors. Highton, having by now seen the original note, published an accurate version in his pamphlet entitled *A Voice from the London*:

> Farewell father, brother, sisters, and my Edith. Ship 'London', Bay of Biscay, Thursday 12 o'c noon. Reason – ship over-weighted with cargo, and too slight a house over engine-room all washed away from deck. Bad poop windows. Water broken in. God bless my little orphan … Storm, but not too ?violent for a well-ordered ship.

Based initially on this evidence, Highton began a public campaign for a better examination of the evidence around the ship's loss. He wrote letters to *The Times* and even published a book of letters and other evidence to try and force the Board of Trade to reopen an investigation. His second letter to the newspaper coincided with Sir John Pakington's speech in the House of Commons and a *Times* editorial sided with both campaigners:

> The chief object of Sir John's speech, as well as of a second letter addressed to ourselves by Mr. Highton, was to show that justice was not done, and that Messrs. Wigram, if not Captain Martin, though 'whitewashed' by the Board of Inquiry, were greatly to blame for the loss of the *London*.
> (*The Times*, 21 Mar. 1866)

This was a bold statement of support, but other major newspapers also spoke out. The editor of *The Standard* accused the inquiry of being nothing more than a genteel discussion of no practical value, and asked how any inquiry could elucidate the cause of the *London*'s loss if it would not admit any evidence that might criticise the owners, who were ultimately responsible for their vessel. Even before the inquiry had finished, the father of Philip Benson, a passenger who was lost, had publicly expressed his dissatisfaction with the proceedings:

> I for one of many bereaved parents and relations am not satisfied that the truth has been or can be elicited in the manner ruled by Mr Traill. The power of direct cross examination is essential to such a result as will exculpate the parties responsible for the trim in which that ship was sent forth to brave the dangers of the Atlantic. I believe that the shortcomings or the avarice of man had more to do with the loss of that ship than the elements, and I have a right to be satisfied on that point.
> (*London Evening Standard*, 6 Feb. 1866)

Highton contended in his letters that multiple professional witnesses who saw the ship would testify to the *London* being overladen and sitting too low in the water. Some of the *London*'s cabins were knocked out to make way for excess cargo, he asserted, and the heaviness of kentledge or ballast had not been properly taken into account when assessing the weight of cargo. His own calculations showed that, if the ship were loaded to a draught of 20 feet, 9 inches, as testified at the inquiry, then the main deck would have been above water level by only 3.5 feet near the foremast. In his published pamphlet, Highton reproduced part of a letter from a passenger lost on the ship, sent from Plymouth:

> By what I can see of it, this ship is going to be a regular brute at sea. They have got her so low in the water that she has no life in her, and will consequently be as wet as any collier.

Highton further insisted that expert advice from many quarters suggested that the ship was too long and too narrow to be stable in bad weather, and that its hybrid design meant it was neither a good steamship nor a good sailing ship. Witnesses advised Highton that the engine room bulkhead was not kept properly sealed all the time on the *London*, so that, when the ship began to be flooded, the stern compartments of the ship were inundated as well, and this would have hastened the ship's end. This claim was explicitly denied by the two engineers at the inquiry, but other witnesses said differently. These were all matters that warranted further investigation.

Highton asked these and many other uncomfortable questions. Did Captain Martin exercise appropriate prudence? Did his financial interest in the ship affect his responsibility for safety? Was he docked wages if the ship was delayed in port? Was the ship over-insured so that the owners made a profit whether it survived or sank?

His aim was to obtain a thorough, searching, and impartial inquiry and he begged the public to assist him in petitioning Parliament. Yet in his pamphlet *A Voice from the London*, published to back up his newspaper campaign, Highton is up-front about the obstacles he would face in securing a proper inquiry:

> It is useless to conceal that I shall have to contend with the influence of a great and powerful firm [i.e. Money Wigram & Sons], which, though it may not be openly and actively exerted, will yet operate as a dead weight against all action concerning the matter at hand. Next to this, there will probably be the indirect opposition of many of their fellow shipowners to encounter; and further still there will, most likely, be a bias on the part of the government in general, and of the Board of Trade in particular, to support their own officers and to acquiesce in the conclusions of a report which, to employ plain language, has simply 'white-washed' everybody responsible for the construction, equipment, lading and management of the lost vessel.

It was an energetic and spirited campaign by Highton and the opposition was formidable. The support from Sir John Pakington – whether coordinated between the two of them or not – was most timely. But would their efforts be enough to secure the vital second, independent, inquiry?

Legal Repercussions

Unfortunately, the determined efforts of Gilbert Highton and Sir John Pakington led to nothing. There was no second inquiry. The Board of Trade simply sat out the bad press and waited for the public to develop an interest in another subject.

Despite all the private reassurance to Traill that the inquiry was not a court of law, the Board of Trade decided for itself that the evidence offered at the much-criticised inquiry offered no grounds for prosecuting anyone, least of all the owners Money Wigram & Sons. The inquiry had concluded that the engine-hatch cover was probably designed, built or fitted incorrectly, and yet no-one was held accountable: designer, builder, surveyor, or owner. Without political support or the backing of a sound independent inquiry, there was little scope for relatives of the deceased to sue the owners either. Eventually, of course, as always happens, the discontent faded into the background: the newspapers no longer received letters about the tragedy; politicians stopped talking about it; and fresh news stories took over. By summer 1866 it had completely disappeared as a contentious subject in the press – no doubt to the relief of many industry and political insiders, but especially the Wigrams, Traill, and the wily Milner Gibson. It will be of no surprise to learn that the changes to the wreck-inquiry process that the Minister suggested would be considered did not materialise.

There were no immediate changes to the law affecting safety at sea either. There was no increase in lifeboats, no tightening of safety checks, or practising of evacuation procedures for example. Perhaps James Traill took some consolation from the fact that, although he had been blamed for presiding over a feeble inquiry, even the recommendations that he had made were ignored: load lines were still not marked upon ships and captains continued to go to sea with their topmasts *in situ*, even when the weather looked like it might turn. Traill may have reflected that he had agonised over it all for nothing. However, shipbuilders had at least been put on their notice to ensure that hatch covers were better designed to prevent them being washed away.

However, the Board of Trade did behave laudably in one respect. Captain Cavassa, the master of the Italian ship who rescued the survivors, was presented with a valuable gold chronometer by the Board of Trade, on which was a suitable personal inscription thanking him for saving lives.

Throughout the whole affair of the loss of the SS *London*, the Wigrams were strangely invisible. At no stage did the owners issue a statement of sorrow for what had happened, thank Captain Cavassa, reward him, or send public condolence to the victims' families. They did not create a memorial to their employees who had died, or donate to the Mayor of London's charitable fund. There is a note in Money Wigram's ledger that the company put aside £100 'toward and for crew of the London loss', although how this was spent is unknown. It was not a generous sum per family, considering the Wigrams' great wealth and that seventy-six employees had died. Later in the same ledger £112 is spent on repairing a carriage and £118 on straw and oats for the horses.

Once it was clear that the Wigrams had evaded prosecution, consideration was given to salvaging the wreck of the SS *London* but it came to nothing. The big ship-owning family simply moved on.

Conclusions About the Loss of SS *London*

Over 150 years after the loss of the SS *London*, it is now difficult to be certain about the events that led to the loss of this ship. However, we do have the benefit of hindsight: we know about other disasters, the evolution of ship design, and changes in the regulation of safety at sea. We can also see beyond the partiality, intransigence, and politics of mid-Victorian England. It is perhaps possible now to make a more impartial or informed judgement about the causes of the ship's loss than the original inquiry board felt able to do at the time.

It is very clear that the inquiry board was right about one thing: the event that made the sinking of the SS *London* inevitable was the loss of the engine-hatch cover. This probably came about for three reasons:

1. Captain Martin insisted on driving the ship into the storm. Had he turned back to Plymouth instead when the bad weather began, or hove-to and sat it out, the *London* would probably have fared better. Either course would have meant the ship avoiding the towering wave

Many factors contributed to the great loss of life when the SS *London* sank.

that subsequently broke the engine-hatch cover. He put the ship about on 10 January 1866 and ran for Plymouth but, at this stage, he probably set the ship heading back into the eye of the storm because the weather deteriorated again.
2. The loose flying jib boom may have helped to prise off the engine-hatch cover, or otherwise damage it, therefore assisting the waves to do their worst. It was clearly the responsibility of Captain Martin and his deck officers to secure that wreckage properly or pitch it overboard, and it looks like they did not do so.
3. The engine-hatch cover seems to have been battened down as best as was thought possible, but its design could have been improved by it being raised further off the deck, being fitted with an iron grating over the top, or being accommodated beneath an extended poop. It wasn't just the *London* that suffered from this problem – the SS *Amalia*, which went down at the same time, also sank because of insufficiently protected hatch covers. The fact that other ships of the time had better protection means that Money Wigram & Sons have some responsibility for the disaster in choosing the design that they did.

So there were potentially poor command decisions, some bad practice by the crew when dealing with loose wreckage during the storm, and a poor choice of design.

The official inquiry noted only the last two of these, albeit in rather circumspect terms that did not point the finger of blame. During the inquiry no significant questions were asked at all about Captain Martin's competence or whether he was at fault. Similarly, although the design of the engine-hatch cover was the responsibility of Money Wigram & Sons, they were not held to account for this or criticised in any way.

Although the immediate event that triggered the loss of the ship was the loss of the engine-hatch cover, there are other factors that contributed to this situation or made it worse, and these are glossed over or ignored by the inquiry.

Some of these contributory factors are associated with Captain Martin, who is eulogised throughout the report and never criticised. He was an experienced ship's master, but of sailing ships, and his officers on the *London* each had even less steamship experience than he did. It is not reasonable to assume that an able captain of a wooden sailing ship will be equally competent when commanding a much larger iron-hulled steamship: it would be rather like learning to drive a car and then being expected to drive an HGV. The Board of Trade eventually recognised that commanding a steamship and commanding a sailing ship were two different skills, and prospective captains had to sit exams for one or the other. It is hard to avoid the conclusion that Captain Martin did not have the right kind of experience for his position on board the *London*, and perhaps this accounts for some of his behaviour.

Captain Smith of the *Titanic* is often condemned for not slowing down as he approached an area where ice was known to lurk, and in this he is believed to have been at least partly motivated by the owner's desire for a speedy passage. Was Captain Martin similarly influenced? Would he have turned back to Plymouth sooner if he had not boasted that the SS *London* would be the fastest ship on the Melbourne route? Perhaps. If he had done so on 9 January then the *London* would almost certainly have avoided the worst of the weather and survived. One newspaper notes that 'In Australia, Captain Martin bore the character of a smart and extremely bold commander, and one who, give him the slightest excuse, would "crack on" to the fullest extent'. If he was driven to try and race through the storm in pursuit of another fast time to Melbourne and push his ship beyond reasonable levels of endurance, then he and everyone on board paid a very high price for it.

The need for speed was impressed upon captains and had become part of the expectation of owners. There is also the potential conflict of interest associated with Captain Martin being part-owner of the *London*, which meant buying into the company ethos and sharing in the profits of the voyage. There is a danger that the owners' interests were put before safety. The public inquiry explicitly *avoided* this point: the names of the ship's owners are given clearly on the ship's registration document but, in the inquiry report, the share owned by Captain John Bohun Martin is incorrectly described as belonging to one 'Edward Martin'. Perhaps it was an awkward fact that would beg awkward questions.

Captain Martin comes across as an oddly uninspiring man. He had a history of sometimes giving up easily, as occurred when he deserted some of his crew in an open boat on the *London*'s maiden voyage. Another commander might have hove-to overnight and set lights out so that a drifting boat had somewhere to aim for in the dark. Several hours is a long time to delay a ship, but not if there are six lives at stake. In this situation, Captain Martin made the wrong decision and gave up too easily.

During the *London*'s dying hours, he also gave up hope and told everyone on board to give up hope, and again he was *wrong* in this judgment. The survivors bear testament to that. He failed to organise attempts to abandon ship – one boat was not launched properly and sank, and the *London* went down with two other boats not launched at all. Captain Martin was responsible for the safety of the ship and, whatever the cause of the ship's demise, he must be held accountable for the fact that so many lives were lost. As passenger James Wilson remarked in an interview:

> It still is an unaccountable thing to me why Captain Martin did not see and have those boats got ready, properly manned and officered, and then tell some of the ladies: 'There is your only chance: accept if you choose'.

To add to this, there is one final point related to Captain Martin. Newspaper reports revealed that another ship, a cargo brig named *Courier*, had narrowly missed colliding with the SS *London* in the Bay of Biscay on the afternoon of 10 January. Some of the survivors saw it, and the captain of the brig reported his close shave in the press. Only a sudden clearing of the weather had enabled the brig's crew to make out the other ship in time, and the *Courier* veered away as quickly as it could, just passing under the *London*'s stern. The *Courier* saw no signals of distress flying and cannot have been far away when the *London* went down. The conditions were terrible, but Captain Martin saw the other ship, so why did he not hoist signals asking for help? Why did Captain Martin not fire distress rockets? Is it just possible that another ship in the Bay, such as the *Courier*, might have been able to lend assistance if it had known about the situation on board? The temptation is to conclude that only pride can explain Captain Martin's failure in this regard.

Apart from the engine-hatch cover design, there were other design questions. Why were the stern portholes and their protective covers not constructed to be strong enough to withstand a stormy sea breaking against them? It is clear that, although the loss of the engine-hatch cover was the cardinal event that precipitated the loss of the ship, the influx of water via the stern portholes made the situation a lot worse and almost certainly hastened the vessel's end. A few more minutes and a second ship's boat might have been launched.

Another design feature of the *London* was that large waves breaking over the ship tended to be channelled towards the centre of the vessel by the 5-feet-high solid iron bulwarks surrounding the main deck. These acted like a funnel and made it less easy for water to drain quickly off the vessel than if, say, the bulwarks had been replaced by a rail or if a better system of drainage had been used. There were drainage channels in the bulwarks called scuppers but, when the deck was awash, it was easier for water to

A humble cargo brig might have saved lives when the *London* was in difficulty.

seek out other means of exit, such as the hole over the engine room. This was made even more likely, of course, if the scuppers were blocked by loose coal. The *London* was built expressly for the trip to Australia, so why did the design not accommodate enough storage space below decks for all the coal that was needed?

With the benefit of hindsight, expert commentators now accept that many early clipper-like ships such as the *London* were over-masted. They carried too many spars that were often too long; they had too much rigging; and their masts were too tall. This made them vulnerable to storm damage. This was contested at the time, but the top ends of masts were often simply blown away and the record of ships damaged in this way speaks for itself. If the *London* had not sustained damage of this nature, then the flying jib boom would not have been brought on board potentially to destroy the engine-room hatch cover. The inquiry report noted that the top ends of masts ought to be disconnected and brought down on deck when bad weather was likely, and this seems a fair observation.

There were other practices in the merchant service that clearly did not help a ship in imminent danger. The great loss of life was clearly caused by a complete absence of rehearsals in abandoning ship, hence the loss of one pinnace at launch, and the failure to launch two other ship's boats in time to save anyone. The *London*'s poor response time to an emergency had been seen in Plymouth when it took far too long to launch a lifeboat and a local pilot drowned as a consequence. A lot of the burden for the failure to get all the boats launched rests with Captain Martin, who failed to inspire an orderly abandoning of the ship, as already noted. But regulation was needed to enforce a regular practice of the boat-launching procedure: crew and officers clearly were ill-prepared. Emigration officers checked that lifeboats were *in situ*, but they ought to have checked that they could be launched properly too.

There were not enough boats on the *London* to carry all the passengers and crew in the event of its sinking because the mere idea of this was seen as impractical and expensive by ship-owners, and some even believed that the extra 'clutter' on decks would endanger lives. Even twenty years after

The solid, high sides (bulwarks) of this passenger ship could trap water on deck if the scuppers are blocked. (Note, in the background can be seen the steps up to the poop.)

the loss of the SS *London*, a Select Committee of the House of Commons concluded that many passenger ships could only carry sufficient lifeboats at 'great inconvenience' and, as is well known, in 1912 the *Titanic* carried only enough lifeboats to accommodate about half the people on board. A change to modern practices had to wait until over half a century after the *London* went down. Meanwhile the inquiry failed to ask why three of the *London*'s precious lifeboats were destroyed by the storm. Could they have been built or stored differently?

Changing the way things were done in the Merchant Navy was inevitably a slow business, because it usually meant extra expense for the owners, who were disinclined to spend more money. They were rich, powerful, and well-connected men; there were a large number of them, too, and their activities were absolutely vital to the British economy. Hence, 'taking them on' was difficult. Another example of long-standing practice with adverse safety implications was the practice of dismissing the entire crew at the end of a voyage, except for a very small number of favourites or senior officers. This meant that crewmen did not get used to their ship, understand how it performed best, or know how to employ the safety equipment. They had to use their own initiative to learn it all from scratch on a new ship for every voyage. Contemporary newspapers suggested that the main reason that captains did not take their mast tops down onto the deck in bad weather was because the raw hands they took on at the onset of sailing were not handy enough to do it. This practice of recruiting a brand-new crew for every voyage arose because shipowners did not want to pay for men to stand around in-between voyages and they saved money by discharging them all. Unfortunately, this mode of employment did not change until 1941.

Did the engine-room crew leave the watertight bulkhead door open during the storm in January 1866? It connected the engine room to space below decks at the stern of the ship, where the propeller shaft was housed. Engineering survivors Greenhill and Jones explicitly deny it, but other witnesses saw it open earlier in the voyage. If it was left open, then the huge mass of water that cascaded down when the hatch cover was lifted off would have flooded into a much bigger area of the ship below decks. This would have encouraged the *London* to settle low in the water stern-first, and would have undoubtedly accelerated the ship's demise.

Finally, although the official report seemed to exonerate the SS *London* of being overladen by its owners, it is clear that no-one could adequately define what 'overladen' meant. The *London* carried a similarly sized cargo on its first two voyages to Australia without getting into difficulty but, on these earlier runs, the *London* encountered no severe weather. Ships needed to be prepared to withstand the worst that the sea could throw at them, whatever their state of lading. Yet experts differed in defining what they thought was safe; professionals observing legally laden ships like the *London* thought them unsafe, and so current regulation was clearly inadequate.

12

The Endings

For many people, the funeral service after losing a loved one is an important part of the grieving process. It allows the bereaved to say a last 'good bye' and commemorate a valued life, and families and friends can come together to support those who are worst affected. When someone is lost at sea and no corpse is recovered, there can be no funeral service, no interment, no gravestone. This can leave a sense of dissatisfaction; of having not honoured a dead person sufficiently. To try and atone for this after the loss of the SS *London*, there were public memorial services and many sermons were preached, as noted in a previous chapter, but some families organised private memorial services too.

Around the UK and Australia, individual victims were commemorated in different ways. Revd Daniel Draper was universally acclaimed by both nations for his Christian leadership, and his devotion was remembered by various means. A memorial was commissioned to honour his memory and placed within his church in Melbourne, where the Draper Scholarship was also established at Wesley College in his honour. In Adelaide, the Draper Memorial Church was built, and in the UK Methodists donated a lifeboat called the *Daniel J Draper* to the RNLI in Penzance, Cornwall. A lifeboat was also bought by the acting profession in honour of actor Gustavus Vaughan Brooke; it was named after him and located at Poolbeg, Dublin. In Australia a marble bust of the much-loved actor was commissioned and given to Melbourne Public Library.

In Melbourne, four linked roads in the Albert Park area of the city are still named after SS *London* victims – Brooke Street, Draper Street, Martin Street, and Bevan Street. James Bevan was a successful and popular businessman in Melbourne, who ran a coaching company. His son, James, lost both of his parents in the wreck, and was brought up near Abergavenny, where he went on to become the first rugby union captain for Wales.

A memorial window was funded by public subscription and placed in St Barnabas' Church, Melbourne, in honour of two other respected residents, John and Emily Debenham. John Debenham was the son of William Debenham, who founded Debenhams department stores, and his

Above left: Memorial to Daniel Draper in the Wesleyan Church, Melbourne. (John Etkins Collection, State Library of Victoria)

Above right: Melbourne businessman James Bevan died on the *London*. (Lithograph by Appleton and Woodhouse, courtesy of State Library of Victoria)

wife's body was the only victim ever found. Over £2,000 was raised to provide for Revd Dr John Woolley's family, and the John Woolley Building at the University of Sydney is named after him.

Numerous memorials were erected to mark the lives of other individuals. For example, a commemoratory tablet to the ship's third officer Alfred Angel – who stood so faithfully at the London's pumps until the last – was placed in Exeter Cathedral, where his father was organist. In Hastings, there is a similar plaque at St Clement's Church to honour second officer Arthur Ticehurst, whose father had recently been the town's mayor; another tablet in the village church of Probus, Cornwall, immortalises Dr Faull, the ship's surgeon. There were memorials to passengers too. Farmer's son John Patrick died in the wreck and is mentioned on his parents' tombstone at Kilsyth, North Lanarkshire. James and Sarah Thomas died on the SS *London*, along with their two children and a servant named Elizabeth Hartley. All five of them are commemorated on James's parents' tombstone at St Chad's Church, Uppermill, near Oldham. The Thomas family were responsible for hiring William Talfourd Salter to represent them at the inquiry.

Sadly, many of the victims came from poorer families and were not commemorated with any kind of memorial. Perhaps most poignant of all is that the half a dozen or so stowaways on board are not even known by name. Some families somewhere in 1866 were left wondering where their loved ones had gone, and perhaps they never found out.

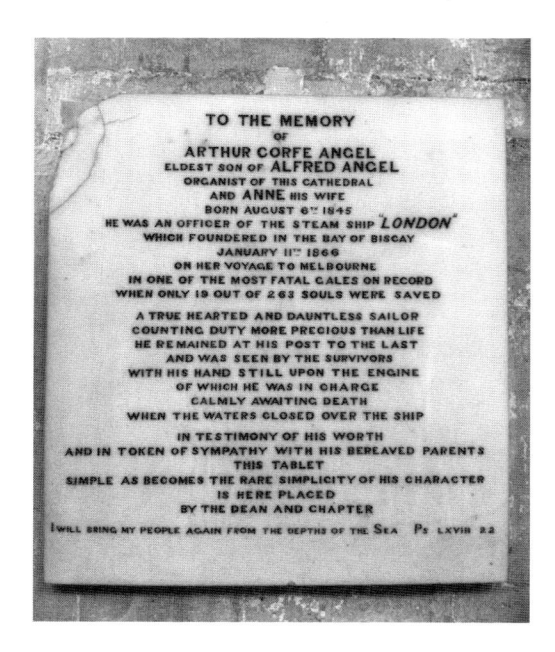

Memorial to Third Officer Arthur Angel. (Andrew R. Abbott)

No monument was ever raised to mark the disaster as a whole, despite the great loss of life and the enormous impact of the SS *London*'s sinking, both in the UK and Australia.

The Survivors

It has not been possible to trace the fortunes of all of the *London*'s survivors, but the lives of the three passengers are quite well documented. Their shared involvement in an infamous tragedy encouraged them to stay in touch throughout their lives. In 1866, John Munro was welcomed back to the small town of Ballarat in Australia with a dinner in his honour. He made a living there as a gold miner and died aged ninety-two years in 1920. David Main's initial attempts to return to Australia were frustrated when, on stepping on board a ship again for the first time, the memories of the dreadful events aboard the *London* came back to him so vividly that he fainted. However, he made it back to Australia eventually and died in Gippsland in about 1910. James Wilson decided to return to Canada, where he had lived before moving to Australia, and set up a successful business in Halifax, became mayor of the city, and died there in 1896.

As far as the crew are concerned, Able Seaman John King also retired to Australia, where he died in Queensland in the 1880s. William Daniels seems to have been put off the sea for life because he never went back to it, instead joining a railway company, where he worked for over forty years. Daniels is believed to have been the last of the *London*'s survivors, dying aged eighty-two in 1922. Alfred White, the youngest survivor, also left the sea, becoming a commercial traveller, as did steward Edward Gardner, who established himself as a barber in Melbourne.

The Endings

John Munro. (State Library of Victoria)

A surprising revelation came in 1897 when a journalist interviewed a survivor of the SS *London* called John Potter. This name did not feature in any list of the survivors. Was he an impostor? The tale Potter told was that, in 1865, as a nineteen-year-old apprentice seaman, he had deserted his ship, the *William*. In order to get another job, he had taken the papers of a friend – James Gough – and adopted that identity as his own. By a remarkable coincidence, another *London* survivor Ben Sheals (or Shields) worked for him at a warehouse and verified his story. Like many of their colleagues, they had both left the sea after their ordeal.

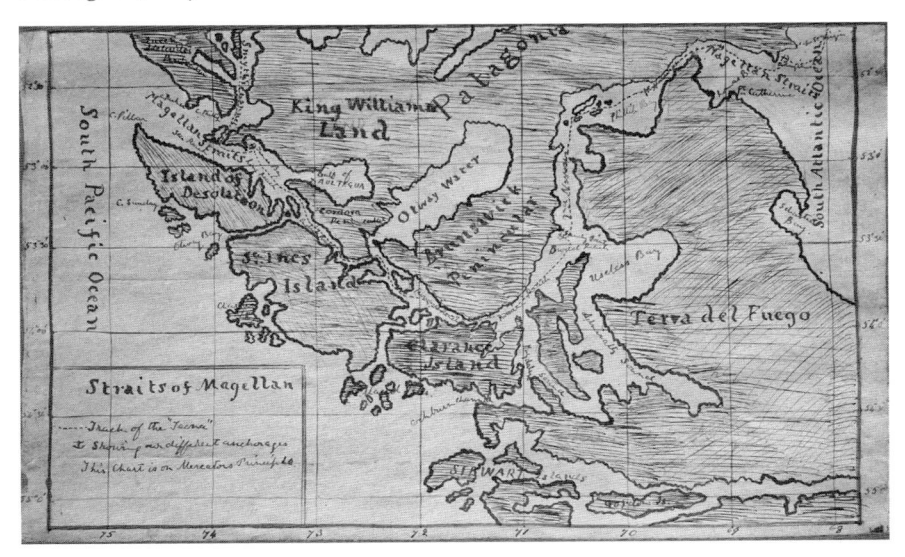

Part of Walter Edwards' hand-drawn map of the route of the SS *Tacna* on its dramatic final voyage.

The young midshipman, Walter Edwards, did go back to sea and even qualified as a ship's master. However, only eight years after the *London* went down, in 1874, he was caught up in another shipwreck. The SS *Tacna* got into difficulties, capsized, and then blew up off the coast of Chile near Valparaiso. Nineteen people died, including all the female passengers, whose lifeboat turned over. Edwards was lucky enough to survive, but unsurprisingly this second wreck was too much and he left the sea to become an Anglican minister. Another survivor of the *London* was not as fortunate. The ship's third engineer, Irishman John Armour, died at sea just two years after his escape from the *London* in 1868. He was only twenty-nine years old.

Money Wigram & Sons

The loss of the SS *London* had no immediate ill effects on the business of Money Wigram & Sons, although the stress of events may have hastened the death of Money Wigram's original partner and brother, Henry, who died in June 1866. The company continued to build ships into the 1870s but business began to lessen because the company would not move with the times. Perhaps the old East India Company legacy was too deeply entrenched. Many of the ships that Wigrams built for others were coastal paddle ferries – hardly cutting-edge technology – and, although Money Wigram & Sons built ships for their own use, they stuck doggedly to the principle of sailing ships with auxiliary steam power. The lessons of the past had not been learned: Wigram ships such as *Somersetshire* (1867), *Northumberland* (1871), and *Kent* (1876) still bore a striking resemblance to the *London*. Meanwhile other shipowners were embracing all that steam power could offer.

In 1872, Wigrams were forced to concede that building ships on the Thames was no longer economically viable and the Blackwall yards were sold off to the Midland Railway Company to form a train depot. When Money Wigram himself died in 1873, the whole business was inherited by his sons Charles, Clifford and Robert Wigram. The company was still heavily reliant on sailing ships to deliver its passengers and cargoes but, in the late 1870s, their old rivals the Green family had gone into a partnership to establish the Orient Steam Navigation Company; this quickly began to dominate the shipping route to Australia by using powerful steamships. P&O soon targeted this route as well and Wigrams began to go into decline.

In a bid to survive, Wigrams relaunched themselves as a limited company with shareholders in 1882, tried to sell off its old sailing ships, targeted new routes, and moved mainly into the conveyance of cargo. This was effective for a while, but it was not to last. Wigrams launched their last ever ship, *Lincolnshire*, in 1891. By this time the company could no longer build their own vessels and had to buy them. The *Lincolnshire*, like the *London* launched twenty-seven years previously, was still a sailing ship with a small auxiliary engine, unlike the full-blown steamships being used by all of Wigrams' major rivals.

ORIENT LINE

FORTNIGHTLY MAIL SERVICE
BETWEEN
ENGLAND AND AUSTRALIA.

AUSTRAL	LUSITANIA	ORIENT	ORMUZ	OROYA
5524 tons. 7000 h.p.	3877 tons. 4000 h.p.	5365 tons. 6000 h.p.	6031 tons. 8500 h.p.	6297 tons. 7000 h.p.
CUZCO	OPHIR	ORIZABA	OROTAVA	ORUBA
3918 tons. 4000 h.p.	6910 tons. 10,000 h.p.	6077 tons. 7000 h.p.	5552 tons. 7000 h.p.	5552 tons. 7000 h.p.

CALLING TO LAND AND EMBARK PASSENGERS AT

GIBRALTAR, NAPLES, PORT SAID, SUEZ, COLOMBO, ALBANY, ADELAIDE, MELBOURNE, AND SYDNEY.

Passengers booked on through tickets for all ports in Australia, Tasmania, and New Zealand.

High-class Cuisine, Electric Lighting, Hot and Cold Baths, good Ventilation, and every Comfort.

CHEAP SINGLE AND RETURN TICKETS.

Managers:—**F. GREEN & CO.**, 13, Fenchurch Avenue,
ANDERSON, ANDERSON & CO., 5, Fenchurch Avenue, } LONDON, E.C.

For FREIGHT or PASSAGE apply to the latter Firm at 5, FENCHURCH AVENUE, E.C.,
Or at the West End Branch Office:—16, COCKSPUR STREET, S.W.

Advert for ships sailing to Australia via Orient Line, which became a significant competitor to the Wigrams.

The end came in 1893: Money Wigram & Company Limited was forced into liquidation. All the ships were sold off to pay creditors. In 1894, the flag and goodwill of Wigrams was purchased from the liquidators by Allan Hughes, who founded the Federal Steam Navigation Company Ltd.

The last of Wigrams' original ships, the *Lincolnshire*, was renamed *Silverton* after its sale, and was sunk by a German U-boat off Tunisia in 1916.

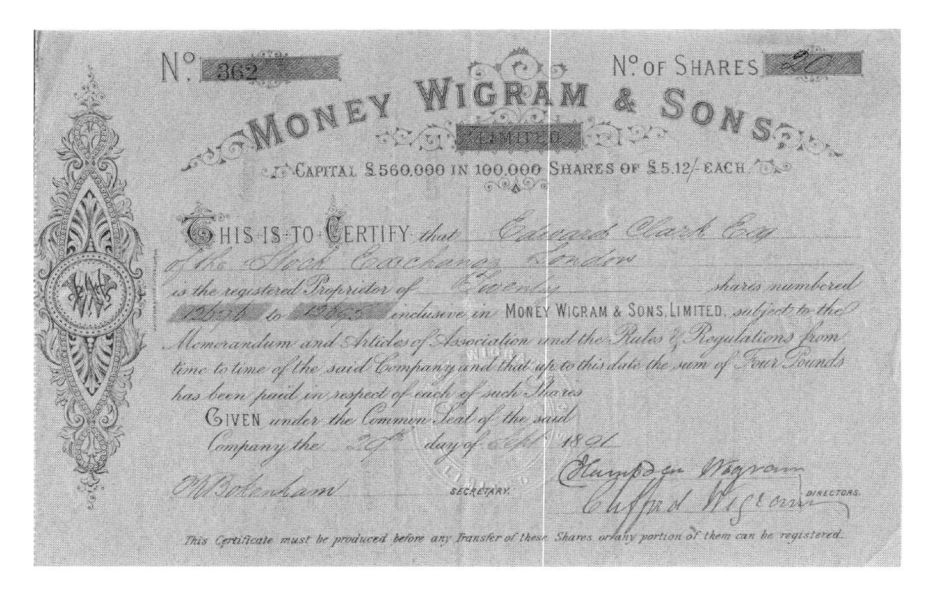

Share certificate for Money Wigram & Sons Limited.

In the late 1880s, P&O were building powerful steamships like this while Money Wigram & Sons' ships still used sailing ships with a small engine that looked similar to the SS *London*.

SS *London*'s Legacy

The SS *London* was one of thousands of British ships that sank with loss of life in Victorian times and they are now all but forgotten – eclipsed by later disasters at sea such as the *Titanic* and the *Lusitania*. However, the *London* was one of a great many losses at sea that led eventually to MP Samuel Plimsoll and shipowner James Hall pursuing shipping reform. They advocated that a line should be marked on all ships to show the maximum depth to which it should sink in the water when loaded – what became later known as the Plimsoll line. Initially frustrated in his attempts, Plimsoll

Samuel Plimsoll.

exposed the fact that a large number of MPs were shipowners or in the pocket of shipping companies – provoking a storm when he called his fellow MPs 'villains' in the House of Commons. Yet Plimsoll was tenacious and he did eventually secure a change in legislation in 1876. It was not perfect, and the law needed to be improved over the ensuing two decades, but the tide had turned somewhat in favour of safety over profit. Shipowners were powerful men and forcing them to accept change was never going to be easy.

One final intriguing detail remains concerning the SS *London*. Mrs Catherine Chapman is mentioned by many survivors in accounts of the ship's sinking on account of her kindness and encouragement. Her husband Henry's utter despair at the news of her death and that of his children is described in an earlier chapter. In the 1930s, Henry and Catherine's oldest surviving son, Frederick – then very elderly – was persuaded to share his research and papers related to Australia's first governor, Arthur Phillip. As an aside within this monograph, entitled *Governor Phillip in Retirement*, Frederick Chapman notes:

> In December that year [1865] my mother opened out to my amazed eyes such a mass of diamonds as I had never seen before. This was the property which 'Aunt Powell' had left or given to her niece my Great-Aunt Fanny, who at the age of ninety-one had given them to my mother, the wife of her nearest heir. Less than a month later (11th January 1866) the disastrous foundering of the S.S. *London* carried this collection to the depths of the Bay of Biscay. In that disaster perished my mother, my eldest and youngest brothers, my only sister, and many of our friends.

So, somewhere within the decaying remains of the SS *London* lies a fortune in diamonds. One day, perhaps, divers may discover them.

APPENDIX

Passengers and Crew of the SS *London*

Reconstructing an accurate list of everyone on board the SS *London* is not easy. The two principal sources are the list of victims in the inquiry report and the list of crew and passengers maintained by Money Wigram & Sons, but they do not completely agree with each other. Additional sources that help to clarify matters are contemporary newspapers, books, and memorials.

All of the crew were supposed to be entered on an official 'crew list and agreement'. However, crewmen travelling only one way or joining the ship at the last minute were often omitted. There were also some disputed areas of practice – were the captain's servants classed as members of the crew or his personal staff? The *London*'s crew list has obvious omissions: it does not even include some survivors. The official list attached to the inquiry report corrects the ship's records somewhat, and various letters to newspapers amend it further. The spellings of names can vary between sources, often because of transcription errors, and where there is genuine uncertainty I have listed both spellings below. There is one mystery – a number of survivors mention the ship's purser, but he is not identified anywhere.

For passengers the task is harder still. Again there is a list that originates from Wigrams, but the inquiry's list has differences and newspaper reports identify various other individuals. It was not considered very important to identify accurately all the lower classes of passengers: hence servant Elizabeth Hartley is not included on any list of passengers, but she does feature on the memorial to her employers, Mr and Mrs Thomas. Many other First Class passengers took servants with them, but we do not know their names: Mrs Traill certainly took a maid, but was she one of the named Third Class passengers or not? We also know that the *London* advertised for steerage passengers, and yet, if there were any on board, they are not named anywhere. Additionally, survivor James Wilson knew of about half a dozen stowaways. Passengers who joined the ship at the last minute, such as Fanny Batchelor, could get overlooked by record-keepers, whereas those who had intended to travel but changed their mind at short notice are included in some newspaper lists of victims when they were not actually on board (e.g., Mrs Hybert; Mr Newton). A large party of twelve were delayed and actually missed the sailing at Plymouth.

Wherever possible I have cross-correlated all names between sources before deciding whether to include them. For example, some newspapers suggest that passenger John Patrick took his wife with him, but a search of newspaper letter columns reveals a communication from his business partner explaining that this was an error – Mr Patrick had no wife. However, survivors' accounts in several different newspapers confirm that William Riley, for example, was a member of the crew, so I have included him despite his absence from the official crew list and inquiry report.

I have not prepared a biography of every person on board, but have added details to the list below if I happened to find them.

Name (variants)	Notes
PASSENGERS (First Class)	
Alderson, Mr James	
Amos, Mr Gilbert Andrew	Warden at Creswick; former magistrate Anderson's Creek.
Amos, Mrs	
Benson, Mr Philip	Twenty-three years old. Brother of Revd Rion Benson, Shropshire. Brother was druggist, Russell Street, Melbourne.
Bevan, Mr James	From Melbourne. Wealthy coach proprietor.
Bevan, Mrs Elizabeth	Née Fly.
Brooke, Mr Gustavus Vaughan	Actor; originally from Ireland.
Brooke, Miss Fanny	Unmarried sister of Gustavus Vaughan Brooke, above.
Brookes, Mr E.	
Brown, Mr T.	Sometimes S. T. Brown
Burrell, Mr William D.	Aged nine. Father Alexander, partner to J. Patrick, below.
Chapman, Mrs Catherine	Née Brewer; husband judge Henry Chapman, New Zealand.
Chapman, Mr Henry Brewer	Aged twenty-four; son of Catherine and Henry.
Chapman, Miss Catherine Ann	Aged fifteen; daughter of Catherine and Henry.
Chapman, Mstr Walter	Aged thirteen; son of Catherine and Henry.
Clark, Mr John	Saddler in Elizabeth Street, Melbourne. Emigrated in 1830.
Clark, Mrs Ann	
Clark, Mr George	Aged twenty-one; second son of Ann and John.
Cutting, Miss Mary	
De Pass, Mr D. F.	Nephew of John de Pass of Melbourne.

Debenham, Mr John	Engineer, Sydney; son of William, founder of Debenhams stores.
Debenham, Mrs Emily Jane	Née Langdon; from Sydney; married 1854.
Dennis, Mr Henry J.	Explorer.
D'Ovoy, Miss [Dovey]	
Draper, Revd Daniel James	Methodist missionary, originally from Wickham, Hants.
Draper, Mrs Elizabeth	Née Shelley, born in New South Wales.
Fenton, Mr J.	Land worker (squatter) based near Mount Korong, Melbourne.
Fenton, Mrs	
Fenton, Mstr A.	Male child of Mr and Mrs Fenton.
Fenton, Mstr T. R.	Male child of Mr and Mrs Fenton.
Hunter, Dr J.	
King, Mrs	Wife of Mr King, a musician from Melbourne.
King, Miss Juliana	Daughter of the above; singer.
Kerr, Revd James	Presbyterian Minister of Armadale, West Lothian.
Kerr, Mrs Sophia	
Lewis, Mr F. [Lewin]	Worked for a bank in Melbourne.
Marks, Mr Edward A.	His brother was an auctioneer.
Maunder, Miss Laura	Resident of Australia, but from the UK.
McLachlan, Miss Catherine	Sister to Mrs Amos (above).
McMillan, Mr F.	Merchant from Launceston, Tasmania.
Owen, Mrs	Sister-in-law of Revd W. C. E. Owen; husband in Australia.
Owen, Miss	Aged four; daughter of Mrs Owen.
Palmer, Mr George Henry	Editor of *The Law Review*.
Patrick, Mr John	Aged twenty-five; of accountants/estate agents Burrell & Patrick, Glasgow.
Richardson, Mr John Ruskin	Aged around twenty-two; resident of Sydney; son of John George Richardson.
Robertson, Mr James	Married with children; worked at warehouse, Flinders Lane, Melbourne.
Sandilands, Mr A.	From a West End firm; survived wrecking of the *Duncan Dunbar*.
Smith, Mr G. M.	Brother J. M. Smith, boot importer Little Collins Street East, Melbourne.
Tennant, Mr T. M.	Civil engineer; resident in London but had worked in Glasgow.
Thomas, Mr James	Of Thomas & Broadbent, woolstaplers, Huddersfield. Memorial at Uppermill.

Thomas, Mrs Sarah Anne	
Thomas, Mstr William Bradbury	Son of James and Sarah Thomas.
Thomas, Miss Annie Mary	Daughter of James and Sarah Thomas.
Traill, Mrs Fanny Mary Stuart	Wife of G. Hamilton Traill, manager of Oriental bank, Australia.
Traill, James Hamilton	Son of Mrs Traill.
Urquhart, Mr George F. P.	From Auckland, NZ.
Urquhart, Mrs	
Woolley, Revd Dr John	Principal of Sydney University.
Youngman, Mr E.	Druggist from Russell Street, Melbourne.
PASSENGERS (Second Class)	
Bevan, Mr Bennett [Beran]	
Brooke, Miss Susan [Brooker]	From Pimlico.
Bruce, Mr Allan	From Greenock; brother ran wholesale store in Queen Street, Melbourne. Brother drowned on *Royal Charter*.
Campbell, Mr G. H.	
Chennels, Mr George	
Clayson, Mr William	Stepchild of Mr and Mrs Wood, below.
Clayson, Mary	Stepchild of Mr and Mrs Wood from NZ.
Cross, Mr George	Compositor from *The Times* about to join the *Argus*.
Davies, Mr Henry [Davis]	
Davis, Mr	
Day, Mr William	Compositor from *The Times* about to join the *Argus*.
Dothie, Mr James (junior)	From Ipswich; been in Melbourne eleven years; married with five children. Salesman for a bookseller.
Eastwood, Mr John Kaye	Miner in Ballarat; son of Michael Eastwood of Farnley Tyas, Huddersfield.
Fenwick, Mr Peter	
Fryer, Mr Francis	Postmaster at Castlemaine, Victoria.
Giffett, Mr E. [Giffell]	
Giffett, Mr J.	
Gough, Mr Charles	Relative of J. Gough, maltster, Flinders Lane, Melbourne.
Graham, Mr Thomas	Aged forty; Thomas, William and David Graham were brothers.

Graham, Mrs Mary	Aged twenty-seven; married just before *London* departed UK.
Graham, Miss Georgiana	
Harding, Mr H. W. [Hardy]	
Hickman, Mr John	Miner in Ballarat; brother was solicitor in Southampton.
Hickman, Mrs Jane	
Hickman, Mstr Alfred	Son of John and Jane Hickman.
Hickman, Miss Elizabeth	Daughter of John and Jane Hickman.
Hickman, Miss Emily	Daughter of John and Jane Hickman.
Hickman, Mstr Harry	Son of John and Jane Hickman.
Johnstone, Mr Charles	
Lemmon, Mr D. W.	Father was ironmonger of Bourke Street, Melbourne.
McLean, Mr Archibald	Plumber; owned the baths opposite the Albion Hotel, Melbourne. Left wife and three children.
Main, David Gavin	Originally from Dartmouth; emigrant to Australia. SURVIVED
Marks, Miss Elizabeth	Aged twenty-three; from Old Kent Road, London.
Meggs, Mrs Ellen	
Meggs, Miss Mary Anne	
Morling, Miss Helen [Morland]	
Munro, John	From Montrose; former sailmaker; miner in Ballarat. SURVIVED
O'Hagen, Mr Thomas [O. Hazen]	
Price, Miss Helen	
Rowe, Mr B. G. [Powell]	
Stone, Mr Frederic	
Trevenan, Mr E. G.	From Cornwall.
White, Mr Henry John	From Sydney. Formerly clerk to detective office, Melbourne.
White, Mrs Annie	From Sydney.
Williams, Mr J. L.	
Wilson, James Edward	From Falmouth, Nova Scotia; brother of Mr B. C. Wilson. SURVIVED
Wood, Mr W. A.	From Arowhenua, New Zealand; Husband, wife and three children.

Wood, Mrs Elizabeth	
Wood, Mstr Godfrey	Son of Mr and Mrs Wood.
Wood, Mstr Thomas	Son of Mr and Mrs Wood.
Wood, Miss Elizabeth	Daughter of Mr and Mrs Wood.
Woodhouse, Mr James	

PASSENGERS (Third Class)	
Barnett, Zulee [Zulec]	
Barnett, Mr	From Russel Street, Melbourne.
Barrow, Mr William [Barron]	
Batchelor, Miss Fanny	Of Union Street, Plymouth. Boarded at last minute.
Block, Mr D.	
Bolton, Mr S.	
Chandler, Mr C. P.	
Clifton, Mr W. H.	From Launceston, Cornwall.
Flick, Mr G. [Flack]	
Flick, Mrs	
Flick, [child 1]	Child of Mr and Mrs Flick.
Flick, [child 2]	Child of Mr and Mrs Flick.
Flick, [child 3]	Child of Mr and Mrs Flick.
Flick, [child 4]	Child of Mr and Mrs Flick.
Gerkem, Mr J. [Serkom/Lerkem]	
Graham, Mr William	Aged fifty-one; tailor from Carlisle.
Graham, Mrs Ellen	Aged forty-nine.
Graham, Ann	Child of William and Ellen Graham.
Graham, George	Aged ten; child of William and Ellen Graham.
Graham, Maggie	Child of William and Ellen Graham.
Graham, Mr David	Aged thirty-seven; had been in Victoria eight years.
Hansen, Mr John [Henson]	Related to Mr Hansen of Whittington Hotel, Melbourne.
Hansen, Mrs Elizabeth [Henson]	
Hartley, Elizabeth	Servant of Mr and Mrs James Thomas (above).
Hay, Mr Benjamin	
Hoyeim, Mr A. [Hogein]	
Jones, Miss Ellen	

Kirkwood, Mr J.	
Lampes, Miss Caroline	
Lampes, Miss Mary	
Lampes, Miss Susan	
Little, Mr John	Aged thirty; fireman on North British Railway; came with Grahams.
McCovey, Mr Henry	
McVittie, Mr David [McNittie]	Aged thirty; blacksmith; came with Grahams.
Miller, Mr Hugh [Millan]	
Morris, Zulee [Zulec]	
Otter, Mr Algernon L.	
Passmore, Mr William	
Reynolds, Mr R.	From Launceston, Cornwall
Rolwegan, Mr George	
Sercombe, Mr John	
Sercombe, Mrs Elizabeth	
Sercombe, George	Child of John and Elizabeth.
Sercombe, Helen	Child of John and Elizabeth.
Sercombe, Henry	Child of John and Elizabeth.
Simpson, Miss Alice	
Simpson, Mrs Selina	
Skeggs, Mr Thomas	
Smith, Mr David	
Smith, Mrs Elizabeth	
Spring, Samuel	A boy.
Trevenan, Mr Richard	From Cornwall; many variant spellings e.g., Treverow, Trevurron.
Umphray, Mr A. [Humphray]	
Walls, Mr James	From Cornwall.
Stowaways	About six known; no names.

Passengers and Crew of the SS London

Crewmember	Age		Where from (previous ship)	Notes
Airth, David M.	24	Asst. Second Class steward	London (First time at sea)	Son of David Airth of the General Post Office.
Anderson, Andrew	41	Able seaman	Heligoland (*Natal Star*)	
Angel, Arthur Corfe	20	Third officer	Exeter (SS *London*)	Son of organist at Exeter Cathedral.
Ansell, Charles	?	Able seaman	?	Signed on at Plymouth to replace deserters.
Appleton, Henry	25	Passengers' cook	London (SS *London*)	
Armour, John	26	Third engineer	Ireland (*Bannon*)	SURVIVED
Arnold, Martin	25	Able seaman	Hanover (*Castle Eden*)	
Bernieker, Johannes	23	Able seaman	Sweden (Swedish ship)	Sometimes Barmiska or Barmura.
Bates, George William	39	Carpenter	London (*True Briton*)	
Bennett, James	23	Third cuddy servant	Hackney (*Childers*)	Sometimes Benwell.
Bramble, James	34	Fireman	Isle of Wight (*Adelaide*)	
Braun, Carl	21	Able seaman	Germany (German ship)	Sometimes Drawn or Brown.
Britsin, Herman	?	Able seaman	?	Same as Herman Hintusky? Not on *London*'s crew list.
Brown, John	25	Able seaman	Holland (Dutch ship)	
Brown, Samuel	22	Able seaman	Sweden (*Natal Star*)	
Brown, Thomas	40	Fireman	Stirling (SS *London*)	SURVIVED
Butcher, James	35	Able seaman	Suffolk (*Constance*)	In Royal Naval Reserve.
Butscher, Hein	26	Able seaman	Hamburg (*Chaa Sze*)	Sometimes Butcher.
Campbell, A.	35	Able seaman	Dundee (SS *London*)	

Care, George	18	Assistant winch driver	England (First time at sea)	And also ordinary seaman, according to inquiry.
Clark, William	23	Trimmer	London (*Shenandoah*)	
Clough, Robert William	14	Midshipman	Huddersfield (*Victoria*)	Son of T. W. Clough of Huddersfield, solicitor.
Craddock, James	31	Sculleryman	London (First time at sea)	
Craycroft, George	21	Fireman	Ramsgate (SS *London*)	Sometimes Graycraft.
Crines, William	18	Ordinary seaman	South Wales (*Edward*)	SURVIVED. Sometimes Crimes or Grimes.
Daniels, William	23	Able seaman	Norfolk (SS *London*)	SURVIVED. Often described as quartermaster. In RNR.
De Horner, August	27	Able seaman	Hamburg (*Chaa Sze*)	Sometimes Dittmer.
Edwards, Walter M.	15	Midshipman	Todmorden (First time at sea)	SURVIVED. Son of Revd John Edwards, Todmorden.
Ellingham, Samuel	26	Able seaman	Yarmouth (*Queen of Nations*)	
Fairbrother, Charles	20	Trimmer	Bermondsey (First time at sea)	
Faull, Mr John Vivian	37	Surgeon	Cornwall (SS *London*)	Obituary in *Lancet* (New York edn) July 1866 p. 429.
Fowler, William	27	Second cuddy servant	Middlesex (SS *London*)	
Funnell, John	25	Servant	Brighton (First time at sea)	Sometimes William or surname Furmell.
Gannon, Robert	36	Butcher	Blackwall (SS *London*)	Left a widow and family.
Gardner, Edward	?	Second Class steward	?	SURVIVED. Not on *London*'s crew list.
'Gough, James' (John Potter)	19	Able seaman	Colchester (*Blue Jacket*)	SURVIVED. Real name was Potter, an apprentice from the 'William' of Colchester.
Grant, Henry		Fourth officer	? (First time at sea)	Not on *London*'s crew list.

Greenhill, John	25	Second engineer	Scotland (SS *London*)	SURVIVED. Sometimes incorrectly cited as chief.
Halford, Frederick	22	Fireman	London (SS *London*)	
Hall, John F.	18	Fourth cuddy servant	Gloucester (*Kaffraria*)	
Ham, Thomas	20	Captain's cook	Bristol (SS *London*)	Married; aged forty in many sources and probably more accurate.
Hanson, Hans Neilson	29	Able seaman	Denmark (*Natal Star*)	Age given as twenty-four in some papers.
Harris, Robert	39	Chief officer/ First mate	Bideford (SS *London*)	Age often quoted as thirty; brother in excise service.
Hart, William	?	Carpenter's mate	Surrey (?)	SURVIVED. Not on *London*'s crew list.
Hayward, William	?	Purser's assistant/ Assistant steward	?	Uncertainty about role. Not on *London*'s crew list.
Hintusky, Herman	24	Able seaman	Prussia (*Cissy*)	
Holmes, George A.	22	Fireman	Paddington (SS *London*)	Some sources George O.
Hoskings, William	29	Able seaman	London (SS *London*)	
Huckstepp, Frederick S.	28	Captain's steward	Southampton (SS *London*)	John or T. G. Huckstepp in some sources.
Huckstepp, Francis	27	Steward	Southampton (SS *London*)	
Jenkins, Henry	23	Storekeeper & fireman	London (SS *London*)	
Jones, David	?	Able seaman	?	Not on *London*'s crew list.
Jones, Henry	36	Winch driver	Bristol (*Orascus*)	
Jones, John	36	Chief engineer	Cornwall (*Bride*)	SURVIVED. Sometimes recorded incorrectly as second engineer.

King, John	28	Able seaman	Jersey (*Valdivia*)	SURVIVED. Some sources Montrose was home.
Lagberg, H.	27	Able seaman	Sweden (*M Miller*)	
Lewis, Richard	27	Able seaman	Holyhead (*Chaa Sze*)	SURVIVED.
Littlepage, Richard	20	Ordinary seaman	Blackwall (*Marlborough*)	
Logan, Edward	16	Boy	Liverpool (SS *London*)	
Logan, Mrs Grace	32	Stewardess	Liverpool (SS *London*)	
Lyell, John	25	Storekeeper and Second Class steward	Sneaford (SS *London*)	
Martin, John Bohun	48	Captain (master)	Westminster (SS *London*)	Unmarried; commander and part owner.
Matheson, Julius	24	Able seaman	Elsinore (*Princess Louisa*)	
Matthews, ?	?	Butcher's assistant	?	Not on *London*'s crew list.
MacKenzie, John	23	First cuddy servant	London (SS *London*)	McKende in some sources.
McKenzie, Morris	21	Sixth cuddy servant	London (First time at sea)	
Merrett, Robert J.	19	Able seaman	London (*Ethiopian*)	Also reported as Memel or Menets.
Morley, John Cornelius	31	Leading fireman	Lincolnshire (SS *London*)	Memorial at St John the Evangelist, Ryhall, Rutland.
Morley, Richard	28	Sailmaker	London (First time at sea)	
Mulloney, John	?	Able seaman	?	Signed on at Plymouth to replace deserters.
Murphy, James	20	Ship's baker	Edinburgh (SS *London*)	
Nilson, Andrew	29	Able seaman	Norway (*Chaa Sze*)	Listed as Wilson in some sources.
Olsen, Otto	21	Able seaman	Norway (*Chaa Sze*)	Alsen in some sources.

Purkiss, Thomas	20	Fireman	Stratford (SS *London*)	
Quin, Edward	22	Able seaman	London (*Castle Eden*)	SURVIVED.
Riley, William	?	Purser's mate	?	Not on *London*'s crew list.
Robson, George	20	Trimmer	Shields (*Tiger*)	
Schlond, John	?	Captain's servant	?	Not on *London*'s crew list.
Scovell, Carl	21	Able seaman	Sweden (*Star of the Sea*)	Sometimes Scovall.
Sheals/ Shields, Benjamin	33	Able seaman	Yarmouth (*Queen of Nations*)	SURVIVED. In various sources he uses both spellings of his surname.
Short, Patrick	19	Ordinary seaman	Belfast (*Sublime*)	
Smith, Alfred W.	17	Fifth cuddy servant	London (SS *London*)	
Smith, Daniel Thomas	28	Boatswain's mate	Woodbridge (*Winefred*)	SURVIVED. In Royal Naval Reserve.
Spurgeon, Joseph	23	Able seaman	England (*Star of the Sea*)	
Staden, John	34	Boatswain	Southampton (SS *London*)	Lived in Blackwall; left widow and five children.
Stephens, Robert G.	?	Able seaman	?	Signed on at Plymouth to replace deserters.
Thomas, Edward	?	Able seaman	?	Signed on at Plymouth to replace deserters.
Thompson, Robert	30	Able seaman	Sweden (*Rockhampton*)	
Ticehurst, Arthur William	27	Second officer	Hastings (SS *London*)	Son of surgeon who was Mayor of Hastings.
Trowbridge, Reuben	39	Able seaman	Deptford (*British Banner*)	Some sources say aged twenty-nine.
White, Alfred G.	14	Boy	London (*Lincolnshire*)	SURVIVED.
Unnamed	?	Purser	?	Referred to by survivors, but not named anywhere.

Margarella, Antonio	40	Able seaman	Athens (*Reliance*)	Deserted at Gravesend.
Fortune, Walter	27	Able seaman	Wexford (*Saladin*)	Deserted at Gravesend.
Rooks, Martin	25	Able seaman	Belfast (*Kent*)	Deserted at Gravesend.
Dougharty, Anthony	25	Able seaman	Belfast (*Diligence*)	Deserted at Gravesend.
Allen, Edward	23	Able seaman	Dublin (*Fame*)	Deserted at Gravesend. Some sources incorrectly list him among the dead.
Johnson, William	25	Able seaman	St Helena (*Saladin*)	Deserted at Gravesend.

Bibliography

Contemporary Publications

Anon., *The Loss of the Steamship 'London' on Her Passage from London to Melbourne: containing a full account of the events and incidents which occurred on board etc.* (Melbourne: Charlwood & Son, 1866).

Anon., *Sorrow on the Sea: a narrative of the shipwreck of the London in the Bay of Biscay, on Thursday, January 11, 1866, with 270 souls on board with a sermon on the melancholy event etc.* (Melbourne: A. J. Smith, 1866).

Board of Trade (editor Farrer, T. H.), *'London' Steam Ship: Copy of Report Upon the Official Inquiry Ordered by the Board of Trade into the Loss of the Stream Ship 'London'* (London: House of Commons, 1866).

Heraud, John A., *The Wreck of the London: A Lyrical Ballad* (London: C. W. Stevens, 1866).

Highton, E. Gilbert, *A Voice from the London and its Echoes: to which is prefixed an address to those who suffered by the calamity and to the public at large* (London: T. C. Newby, 1866).

Jobson, Frederick J., *The Shipwrecked Minister and his Drowning Charge* (London, no publisher given, 1866).

Moultrie, Gerard, *Wreck of the London* (London: S.W. Partridge, 1866). [Note that a second, revised, edition of this book was published the same year with an extra six pages. The same book was also published in both Australia and the USA in 1866.]

Munro, John, *A Brief Narrative of the Loss of the Steam-ship 'London' in the Bay of Biscay* (Dunedin: *Daily Times* office, 1866).

Wilson, James, 'The Loss of the Steam-ship London: by one of the survivors' (*Cornhill Magazine*, Vol. XIV, July 1866).

Contemporary Archival Sources

Board of Trade inquiry and correspondence associated with it is at the National Archives (MT 9/25).
Chapman, Henry Samuel, letter to aunts, dated 18 Apr 1866, Alexander Turnbull Library, New Zealand (Ref MS 8670-088-009 to 015).
Crew lists and log books for Money Wigram ships (1835 to 1860) can be found at the National Archives, Kew (series BT98). For subsequent years consult the Research Guide to crew lists on the National Archives website www.nationalarchives.gov.uk.
Money Wigram's ledger 1858–69, City of Westminster Archives, London (Ref WAT/0789/3/5/1).
Newspaper sources: some are cited in the text, but for others the reader is referred to online databases such as www.britishnewspaperarchive.co.uk (UK; subscription required); http://trove.nla.gov.au (Australia; free access); http://paperspast.natlib.govt.nz (New Zealand; free access).
Ship's registration document for the SS *London* is at the National Archives (BT 108/11).
SS *London* crew list and log book (first voyage 1864/65; no passenger list), and crew list and log book (second voyage 1865; no passenger list): Caird Library, National Maritime Museum, Greenwich (uncatalogued; filed under ship name, year, and ship's official number 50114).
SS *London* crew and passenger list (final voyage 1865/66; no log book): Maritime History Archive, Newfoundland (uncatalogued; filed under ship name, year, and ship's official number 50114).

Other Sources of Information

Crutchley, W. Caius, *My Life at Sea* (London: Chapman & Hall, 1912).
Chapman, Sir Frederick, *Governor Phillip in Retirement* (Australian Historical Monographs No. XL1, 1962).
Lawrence, W. J., *The Life of Gustavus Vaughan Brooke* (Belfast: W&G Baird, 1892).
Lilley, William Osborne, *Bound for Australia on Board the Orient: A Passenger's Log* (London: Andrew Crombie, Hamilton, Adams & Co., 1885).
Lubbock, Basil, *The Colonial Clippers* (Glasgow: James Brown & Son, 1921).
Neville, William Latimer (edited by Caswall, Henry), *Journal of a Voyage from Plymouth to Sierra Leone with Notices of Madeira, Tenerife, Bathurst &c* (London: Bell & Daldy, 1858).
Smiles, Samuel, *A Boy's Voyage Round the World* (London: John Murray, 1871).
Wills, Simon, *Tracing Your Merchant Navy Ancestors* (Barnsley: Pen & Sword 2012).